Fourth Edition

THE ILLINOIS NOTARY LAW PRIMER

*All the hard-to-find information
every Illinois Notary Public
needs to know!*

National Notary Association

Published by:

National Notary Association Press
9350 De Soto Avenue, P.O. Box 2402
Chatsworth, CA 91313-2402
(818) 739-4000
Fax: (818) 700-0920
www.NationalNotary.org
Email: nna@nationalnotary.org

The information in this Primer is correct and current at the time
of its publication although new laws, regulations and rulings
may subsequently affect the validity of certain sections. This
information is provided to aid comprehension of state Notary
Public requirements and should not be construed as legal advice.
Please consult an attorney for inquiries relating to legal matters.

Fourth Edition © 2009
First Edition © 2001

ISBN Number: 1-59767-052-9
L.C. Control Number: 2005920440

Table
of Contents

Introduction 1

How to Become an Illinios Notary Public 3

Tools of the Trade 6

10 Most-Asked Questions 9

Steps to Proper Notarization 14

Notary Laws Explained 19
    The Notary Appointment 19
    Official Notarial Acts 24
    Practices and Procedures 37
    Misconduct, Fines and Penalties... 64

Test Your Knowledge.. 68

Illinois Laws Pertaining to Notaries Public 74

Offices of the Illinois Secretary of State 113

County Clerks' Offices...114

Bureaus of Vital Statistics 120

Hague Convention Nations...125

About the NNA 128

Index 130

Introduction

The National Notary Association commends on your interest in Illinois Notary law. Purchasing *The Illinois Notary Law Primer* identifies you as a conscientious professional who takes your official responsibilities seriously.

In few fields is the expression "more to it than meets the eye" truer than in Notary law. What often appears on the surface to be a simple procedure may, in fact, have important legal considerations.

The purpose of *The Illinois Notary Law Primer* is to provide you with a resource to help decipher the many intricate laws that affect notarization. In so doing, the *Primer* will acquaint you with all of the important aspects of Illinois Notary law and with prudent notarial practices in general.

This edition of *The Illinois Notary Law Primer* contains the groundbreaking law change to the *Illinois Compiled Statutes* requiring the submission of a notarial record for each document of conveyance that transfers or purports to transfer residential real property located in Cook County effective June 1, 2009 through June 30, 2013.

While *The Illinois Notary Law Primer* begins with informative chapters on how to obtain your appointment, what tools the Notary needs, often-asked questions and critical steps in notarization, the heart of this book is the chapter entitled "Notary Laws Explained." Here, we take you through the myriad of Notary laws and put them in easy-to-understand terms. Every pertinent section of the statutes is analyzed and explained, as well as topics not covered by Illinois law but nonetheless of vital concern to you as a Notary.

For handy reference, we have reprinted the complete text of the *Illinois Notary Public Handbook* (INPH) and the laws and regulations of Illinois that relate to Notaries Public. In addition, we have included addresses and phone numbers for the Secretary of State's offices, Illinois County Clerks' offices and Bureaus of Vital Statistics, plus a list of nations that are parties to the Hague Convention treaty, which simplifies the process of authentication.

Whether you are about to be appointed for the first time, or are a longtime Notary, we are sure *The Illinois Notary Law Primer* will provide you with new insight and understanding. Your improved comprehension of Illinois' Notary laws will result in greater competence as a professional Notary Public.

Milton G. Valera
President
National Notary Association

How to Become an Illinois Notary Public

1. Ensure that you comply with the six basic qualifications for an Illinois Notary appointment.

First, you must be at least 18 years of age. Second, you must be a resident of the state of Illinois or employed in the state of Illinois for at least 30 days. Third, you must be either a citizen of the United States or a lawful permanent resident. Fourth, you must be able to read and write the English language. Fifth, you must not have been convicted of a felony. Sixth, you must not have had a Notary commission revoked during the past 10 years.

2. Obtain an appointment application form.

The official application for an Illinois Notary appointment is available from:

Office of Secretary of State
Index Department
111 East Monroe Street
Springfield, IL 62756
(217) 782-7017

If you are renewing your current Notary appointment, you must go through the same process as if applying for a new appointment.

3. Complete the application form.

You must complete the application form provided by the Secretary of State, including the oath of office. Read the instructions and fill out the application, typing or printing neatly in ink. Be aware that any incomplete answers may cause the delay or return of your application, and any misstatement or omission of requested information is cause for denial or later revocation of a Notary appointment. Sign the application exactly as you want your name to appear on the appointment. You must use your last name and at least the initial of your first name.

There is no automatic commission renewal process in Illinois, but you will be notified by the Secretary of State's office approximately 60 days prior to your appointment expiration. If you wish to reapply, you can use the application and bond form enclosed with the notification. If the renewal application is submitted after the expiration date, there will be no grace period allowing you to notarize during the gap between appointments. When applying for renewal of an appointment, you should provide the expiration date and commission number of your current appointment.

Residents of Illinois are appointed to four-year terms; nonresidents are appointed for one year.

4. Obtain a Notary bond.

Obtain a $5,000 Notary bond from a bonding or surety company. The bond must be issued by a company qualified to write surety bonds in Illinois.

5. Send completed application, oath of office and bond to the Secretary of State.

Complete the application; take the oath of office before another Notary or other person authorized to administer oaths; and forward the bond, completed application and oath of office to the Secretary of State, along with a $10 filing fee.

The Secretary of State's office will process the application and mail your commission to the county clerk of the county in which you reside (or, if you are a nonresident, the Illinois county where you are employed or maintain a place of business).

6. Record your commission with the county clerk.

The final step in your appointment as a Notary Public is to register your commission with the county clerk. This can be done in person or by mail. When the county clerk receives the commission from the Secretary of State, the clerk's office will notify you that your appointment must be registered and that the following two options are available for you to receive your commission:

1. You can go in person to the county clerk's office and pay a $5 fee; or

2. You can have the county clerk's office mail your commission directly to you by sending a written request, a specimen of your signature and a $10 check to the county clerk's office.

Remember that your appointment as a Notary will not be effective until you have obtained your commission certificate and registered with the county clerk.

Unless you register, the county clerk will send you two notifications 30 days apart. If you fail to register within 30 days of the second notification, your Notary appointment will be cancelled and a refund will not be issued.

7. Obtain an official Notary stamp.

Before you perform any notarial act with your new Notary appointment, you must obtain an official seal of office. See "Tools of the Trade," on pages 6–7, for the specific requirements of Illinois law regarding a Notary stamp. ■

Tools
of the Trade

Notaries need several tools to lawfully and efficiently carry out their duties. These tools are as important to the Notary as a hammer and saw are to the carpenter.

Inking Seal

An Illinois Notary is required to affix an impression of his or her official stamp — also known as a seal — on the certificate portion of every document notarized. The rubber seal must imprint black, indelible ink and must contain the following:

- The words "Official Seal."

- The Notary's official name.

- The words "Notary Public" and "State of Illinois."

- The phrase "My commission expires _____ (commission expiration date)."

- A rectangular serrated or milled edge border not more than one inch in height by two and one-half inches in length.

Seal Embosser

While not required by Illinois law, the seal embosser is used in many states and is often expected on documents sent abroad. Many Illinois Notaries opt to affix an embossment in addition to the legally required inked-stamp impression. The seal embosser makes a non-photographically reproducible indentation on the document. Because photocopies of documents can sometimes easily pass as originals, the embossment can be used to distinguish an original from a photocopy. Also, embossing all pages in a document together can safeguard against substitution or addition of pages.

Journal of Notarial Acts

Illinois law does not require Notaries to keep journals, but baseless lawsuits may be prevented if Notaries can demonstrate, through detailed and accurate journal records, that they have exercised reasonable care in executing their notarial acts. The journal should include the date, time and type of each official act; the type of document notarized; the signature of each person whose signature is notarized; the method used to identify the signers and the fee charged. (See "Journal of Notarial Acts," pages 40-43.)

Notarial Record Certificates

Effective June 1, 2009 through June 30, 2013, Illinois Notaries are required to create a notarial record for each notarization performed on a document of conveyance affecting or purporting to affect title to residential real property in Cook County, Illinois. Preprinted notarial record certificates contain all of the required information that must be retained by the Notary's employer or delivered to the Cook County Recorder of Deeds. (See "Notarial Record," pages 54-59.)

Jurat Stamp

A jurat stamp impresses on an affidavit the jurat wording, "Subscribed and sworn to before me this _____ day of _____, _____." The stamp is more convenient (and safer, since critical wording will not be omitted) than typing the wording on each affidavit that requires it.

Venue Stamp

The venue stamp is used in conjunction with the jurat stamp. The phrase, "State of _____, County of _____," is placed before an affidavit's text, indicating where the jurat was executed. The venue stamp may also be used for acknowledgments and other notarial acts.

Fingerprinting Device

Effective June 1, 2009 through June 30, 2013, Illinois Notaries are required to create a notarial record for each notarial act performed on a document of conveyance affecting or purporting to affect title to residential real property in Cook County, Illinois. Statute requires Notaries to obtain the signer's thumbprint as a mandated entry in a notarial record. (See "Notarial Record," pages 54-59.)

Furthermore, Notaries increasingly are requiring signers to affix a thumbprint in the journal. A thumbprint serves as proof that a particular individual did or did not appear, thereby deterring forgers.

Many Notaries opt for the convenience of an inexpensive, inkless device that allows one fingerprint at a time to be made.

Notarial Certificates

Preprinted notarial certificates for acknowledgments, jurats, proof of execution by subscribing witness and copy certification by document custodian are available.

Errors and Omissions Insurance

Notary errors and omissions insurance provides protection for Notaries who are sued for damages resulting from unintentional mistakes. In the event of a lawsuit, the "E&O" insurance company will provide and pay for the Notary's legal counsel and absorb any damages levied by a court or agreed to in a settlement, up to the policy coverage limit. Errors and omissions insurance does not cover the Notary for intentional misconduct. ■

As a full-service organization, the National Notary Association makes available to Illinois Notaries all notarial items required by law, custom and convenience. The Association's contact information can be found on the copyright page.

10 Most-Asked Questions

Every Notary has a question or two about whether and how to notarize. But certain questions pop up again and again. These top 10 are asked repeatedly at the National Notary Association's seminars, its annual National Conference of Notaries Public and through its *Notary Information Service*.

As with most questions about notarization, the answer to these 10 is not always a simple "yes" or "no." Rather, the answer is often, "It depends..."

Here is what every Notary wants to know:

1. Can I notarize a will?

It depends. A Notary should only notarize a will if clear instructions and a notarial certificate are provided. If the signer of the will is relying upon the Notary for advice on how to proceed, the Notary should tell the individual to see an attorney.

Laws regarding wills differ from state to state. Some states do not require the notarization of wills, while others allow it as one of several witnessing options. Often it is not the will itself that is notarized, but accompanying affidavits signed by witnesses.

The danger in notarizing wills is that would-be testators who have drafted their own wills without legal advice may believe that notarization will make their wills legal and valid. However, even when notarized, such homemade wills may be worthless because the testators failed to obtain the proper number of witnesses or omitted important information.

In fact, notarization itself may actually void an otherwise properly executed handwritten (holographic) will, because courts have occasionally held that any writing on the document other than the testator's invalidates the will.

2. Can I notarize for a stranger with no identification?

Yes. If identification of a signer cannot be based upon personal knowledge or identification documents (ID cards), a Notary may rely upon the oath or affirmation of a personally known credible identifying witness to identify an unknown signer.

The Notary must personally know the credible identifying witness, who should personally know the document signer. This establishes a chain of personal knowledge from the Notary to the credible identifying witness to the signer.

A credible identifying witness should be someone the Notary believes to be trustworthy and impartial. If a person has a financial interest in a document, that individual could not be a reliable witness.

When no credible identifying witness is available to identify a stranger without IDs, the Notary may have no choice but to tell the signer to find a personally known Notary or a friend who personally knows a Notary.

3. Can I notarize a photograph?

No. To simply stamp and sign a photograph is improper. A Notary's signature and seal must appear only on a notarial certificate (such as an acknowledgment or jurat) accompanying a written statement signed by another person.

However, a signature on a written statement referring to an accompanying or attached photograph may be notarized; if the photograph is large enough, the statement and notarial certificate might even appear on its reverse side. Such formats may be acceptable when notarized photos are requested by persons seeking medical or health licenses, or by legal residents renewing foreign passports.

A word of caution here: a Notary should always be suspicious about notarizing a photo-bearing card or document that could be used as a bogus "official" ID.

4. What if there is no room for my stamp or if it smears?

Usually, if notarial wording printed on a document leaves no room for a seal, a loose certificate can be attached and filled out instead, if the certificate wording is substantially the same as the notarial wording on the document.

If an initial seal impression is unreadable and there is ample room on the document, another impression can be affixed nearby. The illegibility of the first impression will indicate why a second seal impression was necessary. The Notary should then record in the journal that a second seal impression was applied.

A Notary should never attempt to fix an imperfect seal impression with pen, ink or correction fluid. This may be viewed as evidence of tampering and cause for the document's rejection by a receiving agency.

5. Can I notarize signatures on photocopies of documents?

Yes. A photocopy may be notarized as long as it bears an original signature, meaning that the photocopy must have been signed with pen and ink. A photocopied signature may never be notarized.

Similarly, a faxed document must be signed in ink. In addition, if a faxed document is on thermal paper (the slick paper used in older fax machines), the document should be photocopied onto regular copy paper to avoid the fading of any printed matter and to allow the affixation of signatures and the Notary's seal.

Note that some public recorders may not accept notarized signatures on photocopied documents because they will not adequately reproduce in microfilming.

When carbon copies are made, the Notary will sometimes be asked to conform rather than to notarize the copies. To conform a copy, the Notary reaffixes the official seal on the copy (carbon will not readily transfer a seal impression) and writes "Conformed Copy" prominently across the copy.

6. May I notarize for customers only?

No. As a public official, a Notary is not appointed to serve just the customers or clients of any one business, even when the employer has paid for the bond, appointment fees and notarial supplies. There is no such officer as a "Notary Private."

It is ethically improper — although hardly ever explicitly prohibited by statute — to discriminate between customers and noncustomers in offering or refusing to offer notarial services and in charging or not charging fees. However, during business hours and within the scope of an employee-Notary's duties, an employer may prohibit the Notary from charging fees.

Discrimination against anyone who presents a lawful request for notarization is not a suitable policy for a public official appointed to serve all of the public equally. Also, such discrimination can provide the basis for lawsuits. An Illinois Notary does, of course, have the right to refuse a notarization request for just cause (e.g., if an ID seems suspicious or if there are false statements in a document).

7. Can I notarize a document in a language I cannot read?

Yes. As long as the notarial certificate and document signature are in a language the Notary can read, Illinois Notaries may notarize documents written in languages they cannot read.

However, there are certain difficulties and dangers in notarizing documents that the Notary cannot read. The main difficulty for the Notary is making an accurate journal description of an unreadable document; the main danger to the public and the Notary is that the document may be blatantly fraudulent.

Under no circumstances should a notarization be performed if the Notary and the principal signer cannot directly communicate in the same language.

8. Can I certify a copy of a birth certificate?

No. Some states, although not Illinois, do allow Notaries to certify copies, but copies of documents that are either public records or publicly recordable should never be certified by Notaries. Only an officer in a bureau of vital statistics should certify a copy of a birth certificate or other vital public record. A Notary's "certification" of a birth or death record may actually lend credibility to a counterfeit or tampered document.

In states allowing Notary-certified copies, the types of documents that Notaries may properly certify copies of are original personal papers such as letters, college diplomas and in-house business documents.

9. Does a document have to be signed in my presence?

No and yes. Documents requiring acknowledgments normally do not need to be signed in the Notary's presence. However, the signer must appear before the Notary at the time of notarization to acknowledge that he or she freely signed for the purposes stated in the document. An acknowledgment certificate indicates that the signer personally appeared before the Notary, was identified by the Notary and acknowledged to the Notary that the document was freely signed.

On the other hand, documents requiring a jurat must be signed in the Notary's presence, as dictated by the typical jurat wording, "Subscribed (signed) and sworn to before me..."

A jurat certificate indicates that the signer personally appeared before the Notary, was identified by the Notary, signed in the Notary's presence and was given an oath or affirmation by the Notary.

10. Can I notarize for a family member?

Yes and no. Although Illinois state law does not expressly prohibit notarizing for family members, Notaries who do so may violate the statutes prohibiting a direct beneficial interest — especially in notarizing for spouses.

Besides the possibility of a financial interest in notarizing for a relative, there may be an emotional interest that can prevent the Notary from acting impartially. For example, a Notary who is asked to notarize a contract signed by his brother might attempt to persuade the sibling to sign or not sign. As a brother, the individual is entitled to exert influence — but this is entirely improper for a Notary.

Even if a Notary has no direct beneficial interest in the document and does not attempt to influence the signer, notarizing for a relative could subject the document to a legal challenge if other parties to the transaction allege that the Notary could not have acted impartially. ■

Steps to Proper Notarization

If a Notary can convincingly show that he or she used every reasonable precaution expected of a person of ordinary prudence and intelligence, then the Notary has exercised reasonable care — a shield against liability.

What constitutes reasonable care?

The following 14-step checklist will help Notaries apply reasonable care and avoid the most common pitfalls.

1. Require every signer to personally appear.

The signer must appear in person before the Notary on the date and in the county stated in the notarial certificate. "Personal appearance" means the signer is in the Notary's physical presence — face to face in the same room. A telephone call is not acceptable as personal appearance.

2. Make a careful identification.

The Notary must identify every document signer through either personal knowledge, a personally known credible identifying witness or through reliable ID cards.

When using ID cards, the Notary should examine them closely to detect alteration, counterfeiting or evidence that they are issued to an impostor. Do not rely upon a type of card with which you are unfamiliar, unless you check it against a reference such as the *U.S. Identification Manual* or the *I.D. Checking Guide*.

3. Feel certain the signer understands the transaction.

A conscientious and careful Notary will be certain not only of the signer's identity and willingness to sign, but will also make a layperson's judgment about the signer's ability to understand the document.

While Illinois Notaries are not expressly required by law to determine awareness, it is in the Notary's best interest to make a commonsense judgment about the signer's awareness.

A document signer who cannot respond intelligibly in a simple conversation with the Notary should not be considered able to sign at that moment. If in doubt, the Notary can ask the signer if he or she understands the document and can explain its purpose. Or, if in a medical environment, the signer's doctor can be consulted.

4. Check the signature.

The Notary must make sure that the document signer signs the same name appearing on the identification presented.

To check for possible forgery, the Notary should compare the signature that the person leaves in the journal of notarial acts against the signatures on the document and on the IDs. Also, it should be noted whether the signer appears to be laboring on the journal signature, a possible indication of forgery in progress.

Generally, an abbreviated form of a name (John D. Smith instead of John David Smith) is acceptable. However, deviation is only allowed if the individual is signing with less than, and not more than, what is on the identification document.

5. Look for blank spaces.

Although not expressly prohibited by Illinois law, notarization of incomplete documents is cautioned against by the *Illinois Notary Public Handbook*: "Never notarize a blank or incomplete document."

Documents with blank spaces have a great potential for fraudulent misuse. A borrower, for example, might sign an incomplete promissory note, trusting the lender to fill it out, only to discover later that the lender has written in an amount in excess of what was actually borrowed.

If the blanks are inapplicable and intended to be left unfilled, the signer should be asked to line through each space (using ink), or to write in "Not Applicable" or "N/A."

6. Scan the document.

Notaries are not required to read the documents they notarize. However, they should note certain important particulars about a document, such as its title, for recording in the journal of notarial acts. Notaries may also count and record the number

15

of pages; this can show whether pages are later fraudulently added or removed.

7. Check the document's date.

For acknowledgments, the date of signing on the document must either precede or be the same as the date of the notarization but not follow it. For a jurat, the document signing date and the notarization date must be the same.

A document dated to follow the date on its notarial certificate risks rejection by a recorder, who may question how the document could have been notarized before it was signed.

8. Keep a journal of notarial acts.

Although not required by Illinois law, a journal record is a vital part of any notarial act. If a notarized document is lost or altered, or if certain facts about the transaction are later challenged, the Notary's journal becomes valuable evidence. It can protect the rights of all parties to a transaction and help Notaries defend themselves against false accusations.

The Notary should include all of the pertinent details of the notarization in the journal: the date, time and type of notarization; the date and type of document; the signature, printed name and address of the signer; how the signer was identified; and notarial fees charged, if any. In addition, any other pertinent data, such as the capacity the signer is claiming, may be entered. Signers may also be asked to leave a thumbprint in the Notary's journal as a deterrent to fraud — although, of course, a notarization may not be denied strictly because of a signer's refusal to leave a thumbprint.

9. Complete the journal entry first.

The Notary should complete the journal entry before filling out the notarial certificate. This prevents a signer from leaving before the important public record of the notarization is made in the journal.

10. Make sure the document has notarial wording.

If a notarial certificate does not come with the document, the Notary must ask the document signer what type of notarization — acknowledgment, jurat or other — is required. The Notary may then type the appropriate notarial wording on the document or attach a loose certificate.

If the signer does not know what type of notarization is required, he or she should contact the document's issuing or receiving agency to determine this. This decision is never the Notary's to make unless the Notary is also an attorney.

11. Be attentive to details.

When filling out the certificate, the Notary needs to make sure that the venue correctly identifies the place of notarization. If the venue is preprinted and incorrect, the Notary must line through the incorrect state and/or county, write in the proper site of the notarization and initial and date the change.

Also, the Notary must pay attention to spaces on the notarial certificate that indicate the number and gender of the document signers, as well as how they were identified — for example, leave the plural "(s)" in "person(s)" untouched or cross it out, as appropriate.

12. Affix your signature and seal properly.

Notaries should sign exactly the same name appearing on their commissioning papers. And they must never forget to affix their official seals — a common reason for rejection of a document by a recorder.

The seal should be placed as close to the Notary's signature as possible without overprinting it. To prevent illegibility, a Notarial seal should not be affixed over wording, particularly over a signature.

13. Protect loose certificates.

If the Notary has to attach a loose notarial certificate, it should be securely stapled to the left margin of the document's signature page.

Notaries can protect against the removal of such loose certificates by embossing them together with the document and writing particulars about the document in one of the certificate's margins.

For example, the notation, "This certificate is attached to a 15-page partnership agreement between John Smith and Mary Doe, signed December 16, 2008," would deter a loose certificate's fraudulent removal and reattachment to another document.

14. Do not give advice.

Every state prohibits nonattorneys from practicing law. Notaries should never prepare or complete documents for others or give advice on any matter relating to a document unless they are attorneys or professionals certified or licensed in a relevant area of expertise. The nonattorney Notary never chooses the type of certificate or notarization a document needs since this decision can have important legal ramifications. The Notary could be held liable for any damages resulting from an incorrectly chosen certificate or notarization. ■

Notary Laws Explained

In layperson's language, this chapter discusses and clarifies key parts of the laws that regulate Notaries Public. Most of these laws are reprinted in full in "Illinois Laws Pertaining to Notaries Public" beginning on page 74.

In the text that follows, the following abbreviations are used:

ILCS. *Illinois Compiled Statutes*, which contain most of the enacted laws regulating the activities of Notaries Public.

INPH. *Illinois Notary Public Handbook* (February 2003), published as a practical guide for Notaries by the Illinois Secretary of State.

THE NOTARY APPOINTMENT

Application for Appointment

Qualifications. To become a Notary Public in the state of Illinois, the applicant must (5 ILCS 312/2-102):

1) Be a citizen of the United States or noncitizen lawfully admitted for permanent residence.

2) Be a resident of the state of Illinois or employed in the state of Illinois for at least 30 days.

3) Be at least 18 years of age.

4) Be able to read and write the English language.

5) Have not been convicted of a felony.

6) Have not had a Notary commission revoked during the past 10 years.

Application Fee. The application fee for an Illinois Notary appointment, for both first-time applicants and renewals, is $10. Checks should be made payable to "Secretary of State" and mailed with the application and bond (5 ILCS 312/2-103).

Application Misstatement. An application for a Notary appointment found to contain any substantial and material misstatement or omission of required information will be denied. In addition, the Secretary of State will deny an appointment if an applicant has been convicted of a felony or of official misconduct (5 ILCS 312/7-108).

Application Submission. The application — along with the $10 fee and $5,000 Notary bond — is to be submitted to the Index Department in the office of the Illinois Secretary of State (5 ILCS 312/2-105).

Nonresidents. A resident of a bordering state who works in Illinois may apply for an appointment as an Illinois Notary Public. Such an appointment may be made only if the adjoining state allows residents of Illinois to be commissioned as Notaries Public in that state. Bordering states with such provisions include Kentucky, Iowa, Missouri, Wisconsin and Michigan. The term for a nonresident appointee is one year (5 ILCS 312/2-101).

Notary Bond

Requirement. Every applicant for an Illinois Notary appointment is required to obtain a $5,000 surety bond from a surety company authorized to do business in the state.

Filing the Bond. The bond must be submitted with the Notary Public application (5 ILCS 312/2-105).

Protects Public. The Notary bond protects the public, not the Notary, from a Notary's misconduct or negligence. The bond provides coverage for damages to anyone who suffers financially from a Notary's actions — intentional or not. The surety company will seek compensation from the Notary for any damages it has to pay out on the Notary's behalf.

Liable for All Damages. The Notary and surety company may be sued for damages resulting from notarial misconduct. The surety company is liable only up to the amount of the bond, but the Notary may be found liable for any amount of money (5 ILCS 312/7-101).

Change of Name or Move from County. When a Notary Public legally changes a name or moves from the county in which he or she is commissioned, the commission is voided and an application must be submitted for a new commission, including the filing of a new $5,000 bond (5 ILCS 312/4-101).

Oath of Office

Requirement. Each person applying for a Notary appointment must take and sign an oath of office in the presence of a person (such as another Notary Public) qualified to administer an oath in Illinois. A Notary cannot execute his or her own oath of office (5 ILCS 312/2-104).

Filing the Oath. The Notary oath of office is submitted to the Secretary of State along with the bond and application.

Commission Recorded by County Clerk

Issued by Secretary of State. The Notary's new commission will be forwarded by the Secretary of State to the county clerk of the county in which the applicant resides or works. The county clerk will notify the applicant that the commission has been issued by the Secretary of State. The applicant has two options for receiving the commission and recording it with the county clerk (5 ILCS 312/2-106):

1) The applicant may appear in person and pay a $5 fee, at which time the county clerk will deliver the commission to the applicant.

2) The applicant may send a written request that the commission be mailed to him or her. A signature specimen and $10 fee must accompany the request.

Commission Cancelled if not Filed Within 60 days. If a Notary does not respond to the notification from the county clerk within 30 days, a second notice will be sent to the Notary. If the Notary does not respond to the second notice within 30 days, the commission will be cancelled and his or her name will be removed from the list of Notaries in the state of Illinois (5 ILCS 312/2-106).

Jurisdiction

Statewide. A person appointed as an Illinois Notary Public may perform official acts throughout the state of Illinois, as long as the Notary continues to reside in the same county in which commissioned. A Notary may not witness a signing outside Illinois and then return to the state to perform the notarization; all parts of a notarial act must be performed at the same time and place within the state of Illinois (5 ILCS 312/3-105).

Term of Office

Four-Year Term. An Illinois Notary Public's term of office is four years, beginning on the effective date shown on the appointment certificate and ending at midnight on the appointment expiration date (5 ILCS 312/2-101).

Out-of-State Residents. Residents of bordering states whose place of work or business is in the state of Illinois may be appointed for a term of one year, but only if the state of residence allows Illinois applicants to be commissioned in that state (5 ILCS 312/2-101).

Changes Terminating Commission. Certain changes in a Notary's life circumstances can cause the commission to be terminated:

- Legal name change;

- Moving from the county where the Notary was commissioned; or

- Ceasing to be employed in the Illinois county where the Notary was commissioned (nonresident commissions).

Under these conditions, the Notary's commission ceases to be in effect and should be returned to the Secretary of State. The individual must file a new application, bond, oath and fee with the Secretary of State in order to obtain a new commission (5 ILCS 312/4-101).

New Seal. If a Notary obtains a new commission after it has been voided due to changes in a legal name or address, a new seal must be purchased reflecting the new commission information.

Change of Name or Address

Name Change Terminates Commission. A Notary's legal name change always results in the termination of the Notary's commission. In the event of a legal name change, the Notary should return the commission to the Secretary of State (5 ILCS 312/4-101).

Address Change May Terminate Commission. A change of residence or work address may result in termination of the commission (5 ILCS 312/4-101):

1) If a Notary who is a resident of Illinois moves out of the county where he or she was commissioned, the commission ceases to be in effect and the Notary must file a new application, bond and oath.

2) If an Illinois Notary who is a resident of a bordering state changes employment to another county, the commission ceases to be in effect.

3) Address changes within the county of commission do not terminate the commission, but the address change should be reported to the Secretary of State.

Resignation of Appointment

Procedure. To resign, a Notary must notify the Secretary of State's Index Department via certified or registered mail. The official Notary seal should be destroyed to prevent its misuse (INPH).

Illinois statute does not have any provisions for the disposition of journals kept by Notaries. Upon resignation, the National Notary Association recommends that all journals be kept securely for at least five years beyond the last entry date.

Death of Notary

Heirs Notify State. If a Notary dies during his or her term of appointment, the Notary's heirs should destroy the Notary's seal to prevent its misuse (INPH).

Although they are not required by Illinois Notary law to do so, the Notary's heirs should inform the office of the Secretary of State of the Notary's death via certified or registered mail.

Willful Impersonation

Misdemeanor. Anyone who is not commissioned as a Notary Public in Illinois but acts as or impersonates a Notary is guilty of a Class A Misdemeanor. Upon conviction, the person could be fined, imprisoned for up to six months or both (5 ILCS 312/7-106).

OFFICIAL NOTARIAL ACTS

Authorized Acts

Notaries may perform the following notarial acts (5 ILCS 312/6-101, 765 ILCS 30/2 and INPH):

Acknowledgments, certifying that a signer personally appeared before the Notary, was identified by the Notary and acknowledged freely signing the document. (See pages 26-28.)

Administering Oaths and Affirmations, solemn promises to God (oaths) or on one's own personal honor (affirmations) spoken in the Notary's presence. (See pages 29-30.)

Verifications upon Oath or Affirmation (Jurats), as found in affidavits and other sworn documents, certifying that the signer personally appeared before the Notary, was identified by the Notary, signed in the Notary's presence and took an oath or affirmation from the Notary. (See pages 30-32.)

Witnessing or Attesting Signatures, certifying that a signer personally appeared before the Notary, was identified by the Notary and signed the document in the Notary's presence. (See pages 34-35.)

Proofs of Execution by Subscribing Witness, certifying that a subscribing witness personally appeared and swore to the

Notary that another person, the principal, signed a document. (See pages 35-37.)

Other Notarial Officials (Limited to Giving Oaths). In addition to Notaries, the following officials may administer oaths in their own jurisdictions within the state of Illinois: judges, clerks of any court in the state, county clerks, deputy county clerks, the Secretary of State and persons certified under the Illinois Certified Shorthand Reporters Act of 1984 (5 ILCS 225/2).

Unauthorized Acts

Certified Copies. A certified copy is a duplicate of an original document that is certified as an exact reproduction. In Illinois, a Notary has no statutory authority to issue certified copies (INPH).

Weddings. Illinois Notaries do not have the authority to "solemnize nuptials" unless they are also ministers. Only Notaries in Maine, South Carolina, Florida and one parish in Louisiana are empowered to perform marriages strictly by virtue of holding a notarial commission.

Blank Spaces. A Notary may not notarize any blank or incomplete document (INPH).

A Notary also may not sign a blank affidavit or acknowledgment certificate and deliver the signed form for use by another person (5 ILCS 312/6-104[c]).

Declared Incapacity. A Notary may not notarize the signature of a person he or she knows to have been declared mentally ill by a court unless the person has been subsequently restored to mental health as a matter of record (5 ILCS 312/6-104[d]).

Blind Signers. An Illinois Notary is prohibited from taking the acknowledgment of a person who is blind unless the Notary has first read the document to the person (5 ILCS 312/6-104[e]).

Non-English-Speaking Signer. Illinois law prohibits Notaries from taking the acknowledgment of anyone who does not speak or understand English unless the nature and effect of the document to be notarized is translated into a language which the person does understand (5 ILCS 312/6-104[f]).

The National Notary Association cautions against notarizing the signature of anyone with whom the Notary cannot communicate directly. An interpreter should not be used, because the important function of screening for willingness and understanding cannot be accomplished without direct communication.

Change Documents. Notaries are not allowed to change anything in a document after it has been signed (5 ILCS 312/6-104[g]).

Prepare Documents. Non-attorney Notaries may not assist anyone in preparing a document, nor fill in the blanks on a document, other than the notarial certificate (5 ILCS 312/6-104[h]).

Advertising. An Illinois Notary may not use any non-English variation of "Notary," "Notary Public," "licensed," "attorney," "lawyer" or any other term that implies that the person is an attorney in advertising. Furthermore, a Notary may not advertise in a language other than English unless he or she includes in the advertisement, in both English and the other language, a schedule of allowed Notary fees and the following notice (5 ILCS 312/3-103[a] and 3-103[b]):

"I AM NOT AN ATTORNEY LICENSED TO PRACTICE LAW IN ILLINOIS AND MAY NOT GIVE LEGAL ADVICE OR ACCEPT FEES FOR LEGAL ADVICE."

Immigration Expert. A nonattorney Notary may not represent himself or herself to be an immigration expert or provide assistance with regard to immigration matters unless he or she is designated by the U.S. Citizenship and Immigration Service or by the Board of Immigration Appeals (5 ILCS 312/3-103[c]).

Acknowledgments

Common Notarial Act. Acknowledgments are one of the most common forms of notarization. In Illinois, whenever any deed or instrument conveying real estate is to be made a matter of record, the signatures of the parties making the conveyance shall be acknowledged before a Notary or other authorized officer (765 ILCS 5/35c).

Purpose. In executing an acknowledgment, the Notary certifies three things:

1) The signer personally appeared before the Notary on the date and in the state and county indicated on the notarial certificate (notarization cannot be based on a telephone call or on a Notary's familiarity with a signature).

2) The signer was positively identified by the Notary through personal knowledge or other satisfactory evidence. (See "Identifying Document Signers," pages 37-40.)

3) The signer acknowledged to the Notary that the signature was freely made for the purposes stated in the document and, if the document is signed in a representative capacity, that he or she had proper authority to do so. (If a document is willingly signed in the presence of the Notary, this tacit act has the same effect as an oral statement of acknowledgment.)

Representative Capacity. A person may sign and acknowledge a document in any lawful representative capacity on behalf of another person or a legal entity. Specifically, a person may sign in one of the following capacities (5 ILCS 312/6-101):

• For and on behalf of a corporation, partnership, trust or other entity, as an authorized officer, agent, partner, trustee or other representative.

• As a public officer, personal representative, guardian or other representative in the specific capacity described in the document.

• As an attorney in fact for an absent principal signer.

Certificates for Acknowledgment. Illinois law provides acknowledgment certificates for individuals signing on their own behalf, plus a short-form acknowledgment certificate for signers in various representative capacities (5 ILCS 312/6-105).

For an acknowledgment in an individual capacity:

State of Illinois

County of _____

This instrument was acknowledged before me on _____ (date) by
_____ (name[s] of person[s]).

(Seal)   _____ (Signature of Notary Public)

For an acknowledgment in a representative capacity:

State of Illinois

County of _____

This instrument was acknowledged before me on _____ (date) by
_____ (name[s] of person[s]) as _____ (type of authority, e.g.,
officer, trustee, etc.) of _____ (name of party on behalf of whom
instrument was executed).

(Seal)   _____ (Signature of Notary Public)

Identification of Acknowledger. In executing an
acknowledgment, the Notary must identify the signer through
personal knowledge or another form of satisfactory evidence (5
ILCS 312/6-102). (See "Identifying Document Signers," pages 37-40.)

Witnessing Signature Not Required. For an acknowledgment,
the document need not be signed in the Notary's presence.
The document may be signed prior to the notarization (an hour
before, a week before, a year before, etc.) as long as the signer
appears with the document before the Notary at the time of
notarization and acknowledges having signed (INPH).

Terminology. In discussing acknowledgments, it is important
to use the proper terminology. A Notary takes or executes an
acknowledgment, while a document signer makes or gives an
acknowledgment.

Oaths and Affirmations

Purpose. An oath is a solemn, spoken pledge to a Supreme Being. An affirmation is a solemn, spoken pledge on one's own personal honor, with no reference to a Supreme Being. Both are usually a promise of truthfulness and have the same legal effect.

In taking an oath or affirmation in an official proceeding, a person may be subject to criminal penalties for perjury should he or she fail to be truthful.

An oath or affirmation can be a full-fledged notarial act in its own right, as when giving an oath of office to a public official (when "swearing in" a public official), or it can be part of the process of notarizing a document (e.g., executing a jurat or swearing in a credible identifying witness).

A person who objects to taking an oath may instead be given an affirmation.

Power to Administer. Illinois Notaries and certain other officers are authorized to administer oaths and affirmations (5 ILCS 255/2 and 6-101).

Wording for Oath (Affirmation). If the law does not dictate otherwise, an Illinois Notary may use the following or similar words in administering an oath (or affirmation):

• Oath (Affirmation) for an affiant signing an affidavit or a deponent signing a deposition:

Do you solemnly swear that the statements made in this document are true to the best of your knowledge and belief, so help you God?

(Do you solemnly affirm that the statements in this document are true to the best of your knowledge and belief?)

• Oath (Affirmation) for a credible identifying witness identifying a document signer who is in the Notary's presence:

Do you solemnly swear that you know this signer truly is the person he/she claims to be, so help you God?

(Do you solemnly affirm that you know this signer truly is the person he/she claims to be?)

The oath or affirmation wording must be spoken aloud, and the person taking the oath or affirmation must answer with, "I do," "Yes" or the like. A nod or grunt is not a sufficient response. If a person is unable to speak, the Notary may rely upon written notes to communicate.

Ceremony and Gestures. To impress upon the oath-taker or affirmant the importance of truthfulness, the Notary is encouraged to lend a sense of ceremony and formality to the oath or affirmation. During administration of an oath or affirmation, the Notary and document signer may raise their right hands, though this is not a legal requirement. Notaries generally have discretion to use the words and gestures that they feel will most compellingly appeal to the conscience of the oath-taker or affirmant.

Verification Upon Oath or Affirmation

Purpose. In notarizing affidavits and other documents signed and sworn to before an oath-administering official, the Notary normally executes a verification upon oath or affirmation, also called a "jurat."

The main purpose of a verification is to compel truthfulness by appealing to the signer's conscience and fear of criminal penalties for perjury.

Verifications upon oath or affirmation are most commonly executed by Notaries in witnessing affidavits. Normally, what the Notary must do with such documents is identify, give an oath or affirmation to the signer and then complete the venue and the jurat certificate wording on the document.

In executing a verification upon oath or affirmation, a Notary certifies that (INPH):

1) The signer personally appeared before the Notary at the time of notarization on the date and in the county indicated (notarization based upon a telephone call or on familiarity with a signature is not acceptable).

2) The signer was positively identified by the Notary through personal knowledge or other form of satisfactory evidence.

3) The Notary watched the signature being made at the time of notarization.

4) The Notary administered an oath or affirmation to the signer.

Certificate for a Verification. The following certificate wording is sufficient for all verifications (5 ILCS 312/6-105[c]):

State of Illinois

County of _____

Signed and sworn (or affirmed) to before me on ____ (date) by _____ (name[s] of person[s] making statement).

(Seal)   _____ (Signature of Notary)

Representative Capacity. Verification upon oath or affirmation may be taken in an individual or in a representative capacity (INPH). An individual may personally vouch for the truthfulness of a statement as a representative of a corporation, partnership, trust or other entity, as an attorney in fact or as a public officer, representative or guardian. Strictly speaking, oaths and affirmations taken in a representative capacity are the acts of the person making them.

The verification must be made upon the oath-taker's own knowledge. The oath or affirmation is always a personal statement.

State of Illinois

County of _____

Signed and sworn (or affirmed) to before me on _____ (date) by _____ (name of person) as _____ (type of authority, e.g., officer, trustee, etc.) of _____ (name of party on behalf of whom instrument was executed).

(Seal)   _____ (Signature of Notary)

Identification of Oath-Taker. In executing a verification upon oath or affirmation, the Notary must identify the signer through personal knowledge or another form of satisfactory evidence (5 ILCS 312/6-102). (See "Identifying Document Signers," pages 37-40.)

Wording for Verification Oath (Affirmation). If not otherwise prescribed by law, an Illinois Notary may use the following or similar words to administer an oath (or affirmation) in conjunction with a verification:

Do you solemnly swear that the statements in this document are true to the best of your knowledge and belief, so help you God?

(Do you solemnly affirm that the statements in this document are true to the best of your knowledge and belief?)

Copy Certification by Document Custodian

Purpose. While not an official notarial act, copy certification by document custodian may serve as an alternative to a Notary-certified copy in jurisdictions where it is unlawful for the original document to be copied or certified by a Notary.

It should be noted that copy certification by document custodian may not always be an acceptable substitute for a Notary-certified copy, so the person requesting the act should check to be sure that it will serve the required purpose.

Procedure. The permanent keeper of the document — the document custodian — certifies the copy, not the Notary. The custodian makes a photocopy of the original document; makes a written statement about the trueness, correctness and completeness of the copy; signs that statement before a Notary and takes an oath or affirmation regarding the truth of the statement. The Notary, having witnessed the signing, identified the signer through personal knowledge or satisfactory evidence and given the oath or affirmation, executes a jurat.

Not for Vital Records. Copy certification by document custodian is not appropriate for vital records — such as birth, marriage and death certificates — since originals of these documents are retained by public agencies. Persons requesting certified copies of vital records should be directed to the agency that holds the original — typically, the Bureau of Vital Statistics or county clerk in the area where the event occurred.

Certificate for Copy Certification by Document Custodian. In addition to the jurat certificate, the custodian's statement is required. Although not prescribed by law, this wording is recommended by the National Notary Association:

State of Illinois

County of _____

I, _____ (name of custodian of original document) hereby swear (or affirm) that the attached reproduction of _____ (description of original document) is a true, correct and complete photocopy of a document in my possession.

_____ (signature of custodian) _____ (address)

Subscribed and sworn (or affirmed) to before me this _____ day of _____ (month), _____ (year), by _____ (name of custodian).

(Stamp of Notary)   _____ (Signature of Notary)

Depositions and Affidavits

Purpose. A deposition is a signed transcript of the signer's oral statements taken down for use in a judicial proceeding. This deposition signer is called the deponent.

An affidavit is a signed written statement made under oath or affirmation and is used for a variety of purposes both in and out of court. The signer of an affidavit is called the affiant.

For either one, the Notary must administer an oath or affirmation and complete some form of jurat, which the Notary signs and seals.

Depositions. With a deposition, both sides in a lawsuit or court case have the opportunity to cross-examine the deponent. Questions and answers are transcribed into a written statement, and then signed and sworn to before an oath-administering official.

Illinois Notaries have the power to take depositions, but this duty is most often executed by trained and certified court reporters.

Affidavits. Affidavits are used in and out of court for a variety of purposes, from submitting losses to an insurance company to declaring U.S. citizenship before traveling to a foreign country. If used in a judicial proceeding, an affidavit is submitted in lieu of direct testimony. Instead of appearing in court to be deposed, the affiant submits his or her sworn written statement.

In an affidavit, the Notary's certificate typically sandwiches the affiant's signed statement with the venue and affiant's name at the top of the document and the jurat wording at the end. The Notary is responsible for completing the venue and jurat wording, and the affiant is responsible for the signed statement in the middle.

Certificate for Depositions and Affidavits. Depositions and affidavits require jurat certificates. (See "Verification Upon Oath or Affirmation," pages 30–32.)

Oath (Affirmation) for Depositions and Affidavits. If no other wording is prescribed in a given instance, a Notary may use the following language in administering an oath (or affirmation) for an affidavit or deposition:

> Do you solemnly swear that the statements made in this affidavit (or deposition) are the truth, the whole truth and nothing but the truth, so help you God?

> (Do you solemnly affirm that the statements made in this affidavit [or deposition] are the truth, the whole truth and nothing but the truth?)

Response Required. For an oath or affirmation, the affiant must respond aloud and affirmatively with "I do," "Yes" or the like.

Signature Witnessing or Attestation

Purpose. In a signature witnessing, the Notary determines, either from personal knowledge or satisfactory evidence, that the signature on a document is that of the person appearing before the Notary and named in the document.

Witnessing a signature may be used in circumstances where the date of signing is of crucial importance.

A signature witnessing differs from an acknowledgment in that the party relying upon the document will know that the document was signed on a certain date.

A signature witnessing differs from a jurat in that the signer is merely signing the document, not vouching that the contents of the document are true.

In witnessing or attesting a signature, a Notary certifies that:

1) The signer personally appeared before the Notary at the time of notarization on the date and in the county indicated (notarization based on a telephone call or on familiarity with a signature is not acceptable).

2) The signer was positively identified by the Notary.

3) The Notary watched the signature being made at the time of notarization.

Certificate for a Signature Witnessing. Illinois statute provides the following wording for witnessing or attesting a signature (5 ILCS 312/6-105[d]):

State of Illinois
County of _____

Signed or attested before me on _____ (date) by _____ (name[s] of person[s]).

(Seal)   _____ (Signature of Notary)

Proof of Execution by Subscribing Witness

Purpose. In executing a proof of execution by subscribing witness, a Notary certifies that the signature of a person who does not appear before the Notary — the principal signer — is genuine and freely made based upon the sworn testimony of another person who does appear — a subscribing (signing) witness.

Proofs of execution are used when the principal signer is out of town or otherwise unavailable to appear before a Notary. Because of their high potential for fraudulent abuse, proofs of execution are not universally accepted.

Prudence dictates that proofs only be used as a last resort and never merely because the principal signer prefers not to take the time to personally appear before a Notary.

In Lieu of Acknowledgment. On recordable documents, a proof of execution by a subscribing witness is usually regarded as an acceptable substitute for an acknowledgment (765 ILCS 30/2).

Subscribing Witness. A subscribing witness is a person who watches the principal sign a document (or who personally takes the principal's acknowledgment) and then subscribes (signs) his or her own name on the document at the principal's request. The witness brings that document to a Notary on the principal's behalf and takes an oath or affirmation from the Notary to the effect that the principal is known to him or her, and did willingly sign (or acknowledge signing) the document and request the witness to also sign the document.

The ideal subscribing witness personally knows the principal signer and has no personal beneficial or financial interest in the document or transaction. It would be foolish of the Notary, for example, to rely upon the word of a subscribing witness presenting for notarization a power of attorney that names this very witness as attorney in fact.

Oath (Affirmation) for a Subscribing Witness. An acceptable oath for the subscribing witness might be:

Do you solemnly swear that you saw (name of the document signer) sign his/her name to this document and/or that he/she acknowledged to you having executed it for the purposes therein stated, so help you God?

(Do you solemnly affirm that you saw [name of the document signer] sign his/her name to this document and/or that he/she acknowledged to you having executed it for the purposes therein stated?)

Identifying Subscribing Witness. Since the Notary is relying entirely upon the word of the subscribing witness to vouch for an absent signer's identity, willingness and general awareness, it is best for subscribing witnesses to be personally known to the Notary.

Certificate for Proof of Execution. Illinois statute does not prescribe a notarial certificate for a proof of execution by a subscribing witness. When wording is not provided, the National Notary Association recommends the following format for a proof of execution by a subscribing witness:

State of Illinois   )

) ss.

County of _____   )

On _____ (date), before me, the undersigned, a Notary Public for
the state, personally appeared _____ (subscribing witness's name),
personally known to me to be the person whose name is subscribed to
the within instrument, as a witness thereto, who, being by me duly sworn,
deposes and says that he/she was present and saw _____ (name of
principal), the same person described in and whose name is subscribed to
the within and annexed instrument in his/her authorized capacity(ies) as
a party thereto, execute the same, and that said affiant subscribed his/her
name to the within instrument as a witness at the request of _____
(name of principal).

(Seal)   _____ (Signature of Notary)

PRACTICES AND PROCEDURES

Identifying Document Signers

Satisfactory Evidence. Under Illinois law, every individual
whose signature is notarized must be positively identified
by the Notary Public. Each of the following three methods
of identification is considered "satisfactory evidence" of an
individual's identity (5 ILCS 312/6-102):

1) The Notary's personal knowledge of the signer's identity.
(See "Personal Knowledge of Identity," below.)

2) Effective June 1, 2009, through June 30, 2013, reliable
identification documents or ID cards as defined by statute.
(See "Identification Documents," pages 38–39.)

3) The oath or affirmation of a personally known credible
identifying witness. (See "Credible Identifying Witnesses,"
pages 39–40.)

Personal Knowledge of Identity

Definition. The safest and most reliable method of identifying
a document signer is for the Notary to depend upon his or
her own personal knowledge of the signer's identity. Personal
knowledge means familiarity with an individual resulting from
interactions with that person over a period of time sufficient to
eliminate every reasonable doubt that the person has the identity
claimed. The familiarity should come from association with the
individual in relation to other people and should be based upon

a chain of circumstances surrounding the individual.

Illinois law does not specify how long a Notary must be acquainted with an individual before personal knowledge of identity may be claimed. The Notary's common sense must prevail. In general, the longer the Notary is acquainted with a person, and the more interactions the Notary has had with that person, the more likely the individual is personally known.

For instance, the Notary might safely regard a friend since childhood as personally known, but would be foolish to consider a person met for the first time the previous day as such. Whenever the Notary has a reasonable doubt about a signer's identity, that individual should be considered not personally known, and the identification should be made through either a credible identifying witness or reliable identification documents.

Identification Documents

Acceptable Identification Documents. Effective June 1, 2009 through June 30, 2013, Illinois law requires that an identification document used to identify a signer for a notarial act be valid at the time of notarization, issued by a state or federal government agency and contain a photograph and signature of the bearer (5 ILCS 312/6-102[d][3]).

Acceptable identification documents include the following:

- Illinois driver's license or non-driver's ID

- Driver's license or identification card from another U.S. state, territory or jurisdiction

- Foreign passport stamped for entry into the U.S. by the United States Citizenship and Immigration Services (USCIS)

- U.S. military ID card

- ID card issued by the USCIS

Unacceptable Identification Documents. Examples of unacceptable identification documents include Social Security cards, birth certificates and credit cards. Social Security cards and birth certificates, while issued by the government, do not bear a photograph of the bearer. Credit cards, while they may contain signatures and a photograph of the individual, are not issued by the government.

Multiple Identification. While one good identification document or card is sufficient to identify a signer, the Notary may ask for more.

Fraudulent Identification. Identification documents are the least secure of the three methods of identifying a document signer, because phony ID cards are common. The Notary should scrutinize each card for evidence of tampering or counterfeiting, or for evidence that it is a genuine card that has been issued to an impostor.

Some clues that an ID card may have been fraudulently tampered with include: mismatched type styles, a photograph raised from the surface, a signature that does not match the signature on the document, unauthorized lamination of the card and smudges, erasures, smears and discolorations.

Possible tip-offs to a counterfeit ID card include: misspelled words, a brand new-looking card with an old date of issuance, two cards with exactly the same photograph and inappropriate patterns and textures.

Some possible indications that a card may have been issued to an impostor include: the birth date or address on the card is unknown to the bearer, all ID cards seem brand new and the bearer is unwilling to leave a thumbprint in the journal. (Such a print is not a requirement of law but is requested by some Notaries as protection against forgers and lawsuits. Refusal to leave a thumbprint is not in itself grounds to deny a notarization.)

Credible Identifying Witnesses

Purpose. When a document signer is not personally known to the Notary and is not able to present reliable ID cards, that signer may be identified on the oath (or affirmation) of a credible identifying witness.

Qualifications. Illinois law requires that a credible identifying witness be personally known to the Notary. In addition, the National Notary Association strongly recommends that the document signer also be personally known to the credible identifying witness. Thus, there should be a chain of personal knowledge from the Notary to the credible identifying witness to the signer. In a sense, a credible identifying witness is a walking, talking ID card (5 ILCS 312/6-102[d]).

A reliable credible identifying witness should have a reputation for honesty. The witness should be a competent individual who will not be tricked, cajoled, bullied or otherwise influenced into identifying someone he or she does not really know. In addition, the witness should have no personal interest in the transaction.

Oath (Affirmation) for Credible Identifying Witness. An oath or affirmation must be administered to the credible identifying witness by the Notary to compel truthfulness.

If not otherwise prescribed by Illinois law, an acceptable credible-witness oath or affirmation might be:

> Do you solemnly swear you know that this signer is the person he/she claims to be, so help you God?

> (Do you solemnly affirm you know that this signer is the person he/she claims to be?)

Signature in Notary's Journal. If the Notary maintains a journal — although a journal is not required by law — each credible identifying witness should sign the Notary's journal along with the document signer. The Notary should also print each witness's name and address.

Journal of Notarial Acts

Recommended. The National Notary Association and many Notary-regulating officials across the nation strongly recommend that every Notary keep a detailed, accurate and sequential journal of notarial acts, although not required by law in Illinois.

Prudent Notaries keep detailed and accurate journals of their notarial acts for many reasons:

- Keeping records is a businesslike practice that every conscientious businessperson and public official should engage in. Not keeping records of important transactions, whether private or public, is risky.

- A Notary's record book protects the public's rights to valuable property and to due process by providing documentary evidence in the event a document is lost or altered, or if a transaction is later challenged.

• In the event of a civil lawsuit alleging that the Notary's negligence or misconduct caused the plaintiff financial harm, a detailed journal of notarial acts can protect the Notary by showing that reasonable care was used to identify a signer. It would be difficult to contend that the Notary did not bother to identify a signer if the Notary's journal contains a detailed description of the ID cards that the signer presented.

• Since civil lawsuits arising from a contested notarial act typically take place three to six years after the act occurs, the Notary normally cannot accurately testify in court about the particulars of a notarization without a journal to aid his or her memory.

• Journals of notarial acts can prevent or abort baseless lawsuits by showing that a Notary did use reasonable care, or that a transaction did occur as recorded. Journal fingerprints and signatures are especially effective in defeating such groundless suits.

• Requiring each document signer to leave a signature, or even a thumbprint, in the Notary's journal both deters attempted forgeries and provides strong evidence for a conviction should a forgery occur.

Journal Entries. The Notary's journal should contain the following information for each notarial act performed:

1) The date, time of day and type of notarization (e.g., jurat, acknowledgment, etc.).

2) The type (or title) of document notarized (e.g., deed of trust, power of attorney, etc.), including the number of pages and the date of the document.

3) The signature, address and printed name of each document signer and any witnesses.

4) A statement as to how the signer was identified. If by personal knowledge, the journal entry should read "Personal Knowledge." If by satisfactory evidence, the journal entry should contain either a description of the ID card accepted, including the type of ID, the government

agency issuing the ID, the serial or identifying number and the date of issuance or expiration; or the signature of any credible identifying witness and how that credible identifying witness was identified. (See "Credible Identifying Witness," pages 39–40.)

5) The fee charged for the notarial service.

Additional Entries. Notaries may include additional information in the journal that is pertinent to a given notarization. Many Notaries, for example, enter the telephone number of all signers and witnesses, as well as the address where the notarization was performed, if not at the Notary's office. A description of the document signer's demeanor (e.g., "The signer appeared very nervous") or notations about the identity of other persons who were present for the notarization may also be applicable.

One important entry to include is the signer's representative capacity — whether the signer is acting as attorney in fact, trustee, guardian, corporate officer or in another capacity — if not signing on his or her own behalf.

Journal Thumbprint. Increasingly, Notaries are asking document signers to leave a thumbprint in the journal. The journal thumbprint is a strong deterrent to forgery, because it represents absolute proof of the forger's identity and appearance. Nothing prevents a Notary from asking for a thumbprint for every notarial act, if the signer is willing. However, the Notary may not make leaving a thumbprint a precondition for notarizing.

Complete Entry Before Certificate. The Notary should complete the journal entry before filling out the notarial certificate on a document to prevent the signer from leaving with the notarized document before vital information is entered in the journal.

Never Surrender Journal. Notaries should never surrender control of their journals to anyone, unless expressly subpoenaed by a court order. Even when an employer has paid for the Notary's official journal and stamp, they go with the Notary upon termination of employment; no person but the Notary may lawfully possess and write in these records.

Inspection of Notary Journal. Since the Notary's official journal is kept for the public benefit, members of the public may lawfully request to examine it.

The careful Notary will only show and provide copies of entries upon presentation of a signed and written request that includes each signer(s) name(s), type of document and month and year of notarization. In addition, the National Notary Association recommends that the individual requesting the copy be positively identified and sign the Notary's journal.

Although the journal may be inspected, the Notary should take steps to ensure its security and the privacy of information contained in it. Any inspection must be performed in the Notary's presence. No one should be allowed to take possession of the journal, even for just a few minutes.

During inspection of the journal, the conscientious Notary will protect the confidentiality of document signers and transactions recorded in the journal that are not the subject of the inspection. The Notary may cover over these entries with a blank piece of paper, thereby ensuring only the requested entry or entries are viewed.

Notarial Certificate

Requirement. In notarizing any document, a Notary must complete a notarial certificate. The certificate is wording that indicates exactly what the Notary has certified. The notarial certificate wording may either be printed on the document or on an attachment to it. The certificate should contain:

1) A venue indicating where the notarization is being performed. "State of Illinois, County of _____," is the typical venue wording, with the county name inserted in the blank. The letters "SS." or "SCT." sometimes appear after the venue; they abbreviate the traditional Latin word *scilicet*, meaning "in particular" or "namely."

2) A statement of particulars indicating what the notarization has attested to. An acknowledgment certificate would include such wording as:

"On ____ (date) before me, _____ (name of Notary), personally appeared, _____ (name of signer), personally known to me (or proved to me on the basis of satisfactory evidence) to be the person(s) ..."

A jurat certificate would include such wording as:

"Subscribed and sworn to (or affirmed) before me on this _____ day of _____ (month), _____ (year), by _____."

3) A testimonium clause, which may be optional if the date is included in the statement of particulars:

"Witness my hand and official seal, this _____ day of _____, _____."

In this phrase, the Notary formally attests to the truthfulness of the preceding facts in the certificate. "Hand" means signature.

4) The official signature of the Notary, exactly as the name appears on the Notary's commission (INPH).

5) The official seal of the Notary. On many certificates, the letters "L.S." appear, indicating where the Notary's stamp or seal is to be affixed. These letters abbreviate the Latin term *locus sigilli*, meaning "place of the seal." An inking seal should be placed near but not over the letters so that wording imprinted by the seal will not be obscured. An embossing seal, used in conjunction with an inking seal, may be placed directly over the letters — slightly displacing portions of the characters and leaving a clue that document examiners can use to distinguish an original from a forged photocopy.

Loose Certificates. When appropriate certificate wording is not preprinted on the document, a loose certificate may be attached by the Notary. Normally, this form is stapled to the document's left margin on the signature page. Only one side of the certificate should be stapled, so it can be lifted to view the document underneath.

To prevent a loose certificate from being removed and fraudulently placed on another document, there are precautions a Notary can take. The Notary can emboss the certificate and document together, writing, "Attached document bears embossment," on the certificate. Or the Notary can write a brief description of the document on the certificate: e.g.,

"This certificate is attached to a _____ (title or type of document), dated _____, of _____ (number) pages, also signed by _____ (name[s] of other signer[s])."

While fraud-deterrent steps can make it much more difficult for a loose certificate to be removed and misused, there is no absolute protection against removal and misuse. However, Notaries must ensure that while a certificate remains in their control, it is attached only to its intended document.

Do Not Pre-Sign/Pre-Seal Certificates. A Notary should never sign and/or seal certificates ahead of time or permit other persons to attach loose notarial certificates to documents. Nor should the Notary send an unattached, signed and sealed, loose certificate through the mail, even if requested to do so by a signer who previously appeared before the Notary. These actions may facilitate fraud or forgery, and they could subject the Notary to lawsuits to recover damages resulting from the Notary's neglect or misconduct.

Selecting Certificates. It is not the role of the Notary to decide what type of certificate — thus, what type of notarization — a document needs. As ministerial officials, Notaries follow instructions and fill out forms that have been provided for them; they do not issue instructions or decide which forms are appropriate in a given case.

If a document is presented to a Notary without certificate wording and the signer does not know what type of notarization is appropriate, the signer should be asked to find out what kind of notarization and certificate are needed. Usually, the agency that issued the document or the one that will be accepting the document can provide this information. Selecting certificates may be considered the unauthorized practice of law.

Notary Seal

Requirement. An Illinois Notary must affix an impression of an official seal on the certificate portion of every document notarized. The impression should be placed near the Notary's signature on a certificate and should not be placed over any signature or wording on a notarial certificate (5 ILCS 312/3-101).

Inking Stamp. The official seal must be a rubber stamp that imprints indelible, black ink to be photographically reproducible (INPH).

Format. The Illinois Notary stamp must be rectangular, not larger than 1 inch by 2½ inches, with a serrated or milled edge border (INPH).

Required Information. The Notary stamp must contain the following elements (5 ILCS 312/3-101):

1) The words "Official Seal."

2) The Notary's name exactly as it appears on the Notary's commission.

3) The words "Notary Public," "State of Illinois" and "My commission expires _____ (commission expiration date)."

Illinois law neither requires nor prohibits the name of the county to appear on the stamp (INPH).

L.S. The letters "L.S." — abbreviating the Latin term *locus sigilli*, meaning "location of the seal" — appear on many notarial certificates to indicate where the Notary seal should be placed. While an embossing seal may be affixed over these letters, an inking stamp should be imprinted near, but not over, the letters.

Placement of the Stamp Impression. The Notary's official stamp impression should be placed near the Notary's signature on the notarial certificate.

The Notary may not affix the stamp over any text on the document or certificate, not even standard or boilerplate clauses. Some recorders will reject documents if writing or document text intrudes within the borders of the Notary's stamp or seal. If there is no room for a stamp, the Notary may have no choice but to complete and attach a loose certificate that duplicates the notarial wording on the document.

Personal Property. The stamp — along with the journal and the Notary's certificate of appointment — is considered the personal property of the Notary, regardless of who paid for the commission or stamp. It should never be surrendered to an employer upon termination of employment.

Wrongful Possession. Anyone who has unlawful possession of a Notary's official seal is guilty of a misdemeanor. Conviction may carry a fine of up to $1,000 (5 ILCS 312/7-107).

Destroy When Commission Terminates. When the Notary's commission terminates, whether through revocation, resignation or death, the Notary or the Notary's heirs should destroy or deface the seal to prevent it from being misused (INPH).

Fees for Notarial Acts

Maximum Fees. The following maximum fees for performing notarial acts are allowed by Illinois law (5 ILCS 312/3-104):

Acknowledgments — $1. For taking an acknowledgment, the Notary may charge no more than $1 for each signature notarized.

Oaths and Affirmations Without Signature — $1. For administering an oath or affirmation without requiring the oath-taker or affirmant to sign a document, the Notary may charge no more than $1 per oath or affirmation.

Verification Upon Oath or Affirmation — $1. For executing a jurat on an affidavit or other form of verification upon oath or affirmation, the Notary may charge no more than $1 for each signature. (This fee includes administration of the oath or affirmation.)

All Other Notarial Acts — $1. For performing any other notarial act or for completing a certificate and seal not otherwise provided for, the Notary may charge $1.

Fees for Immigration Forms. Notaries who are designated entities by the U.S. Citizenship and Immigration Service may charge for filling out immigration forms. The maximum fees are as follows (5 ILCS 312/3-104[b]):

- $10 per immigration form

- $10 per page for performing required translations on immigration forms

- $1 for performing a notarization

- $3 for obtaining a document required to complete an immigration form

The maximum fee is $75 per person for a complete application, up to 4 persons per immediate family.

Fee for Notarial Record. Effective June 1, 2009 through June 30, 2013, Illinois Notaries may charge up to $25 for performing any notarial act that requires completion of a notarial record in connection to a document of conveyance that transfers, or purports to transfer, title to residential real property located in Cook County (5 ILCS 312/3-104[a]). (See "Notarial Record," pages 54-60.)

Records and Receipts for Fees. Notaries must keep records of fees accepted for notarial services provided. In addition, Notaries must provide a receipt for any fee accepted in the performance of a notarial act (5 ILCS 312/3-104[d]).

Option Not to Charge. Notaries are not required to charge for their notarial services, and they may charge any fee less than the statutory maximum (INPH).

Travel Fees. Charges for travel by a Notary are not specified by law. Such fees are proper only if the Notary and signer agree beforehand on the amount to be charged. The signer must understand that a travel fee is not stipulated in law and is separate from the notarial fees described above.

Post Fee Schedule with Non-English Ads. Any advertisement for notarial services in a language other than English must contain a schedule of fees (5 ILCS 312/3-103).

Overcharging. If a Notary charges more than the legally prescribed fees, he or she may be guilty of a misdemeanor for the first offense. If a second offense is committed within five years of the previous conviction, the Notary may be guilty of a Class 3 Felony. In addition, the Attorney General or any state's attorney may bring action against the violator and civil action may be brought as well (5 ILCS 312/3-104).

Disqualifying Interest

Impartiality. Notaries are appointed by the state to be impartial, disinterested witnesses whose screening duties help ensure the integrity of important legal and commercial transactions. Lack of impartiality by a Notary throws doubt on the integrity and lawfulness of any transaction. A Notary must never notarize his or her own signature, or notarize in a transaction in which the Notary has a financial or beneficial interest.

Illinois statutes specify that a Notary may not notarize any instrument in which the Notary's name appears as a party to the transaction (5 ILCS 312/6-104[b]).

Financial or Beneficial Interest. A prudent Notary will not perform any notarization related to a transaction in which that Notary or the Notary's spouse has a direct financial or beneficial interest. A financial or beneficial interest exists when the Notary or the Notary's spouse is named as a principal in a financial transaction or when the Notary receives an advantage, right, privilege, property or fee valued in excess of the lawfully prescribed notarial fee.

In regard to real estate transactions, a Notary is generally considered to have a disqualifying financial or beneficial interest when that Notary or the Notary's spouse is a grantor or grantee, mortgagor or mortgagee, trustor or trustee, lessor or lessee or a beneficiary of the transaction.

Relatives. Illinois Notaries are not prohibited from notarizing for spouses, children or other relatives (INPH).

The National Notary Association strongly discourages Notaries from notarizing for persons related by blood or marriage because of the likelihood of a financial or beneficial interest, whether large or small.

Unauthorized Practice of Law

Do Not Assist Others with Legal Matters. As a ministerial officer, the nonattorney Notary is generally not permitted to assist other persons in drafting, preparing, selecting, completing or understanding a document or transaction (5 ILCS 312/6-104[h] and 312/7-109).

The Notary should not fill in the blanks on a document for other persons, tell others what document they need, how to draft it nor advise others about the legal sufficiency of a document, and especially not for a fee.

A Notary may fill in the blanks on the portion of any document containing the notarial certificate. And a Notary, as a private individual, may prepare legal documents that he or she is personally a party to. However, the Notary may not then notarize his or her signature on these same documents.

Notaries who overstep their authority by advising others on legal matters may have their appointments revoked and may be prosecuted for the unauthorized practice of law.

A Notary who is not an attorney or accredited immigration representative who accepts a fee for providing legal advice may be held liable for three times the amount charged or a minimum fine of $1,001, and restitution of the amount paid to the consumer. Additional civil or criminal penalties may also apply (5 ILCS 312/3-103[f]).

Exceptions. Nonattorney Notaries who are specially trained, certified or licensed in a particular field (e.g., real estate, insurance and escrow) may advise others about documents in that field, but in no other. In addition, trained paralegals under the supervision of an attorney may advise others about documents in legal matters.

Signature by Mark

Mark Serves as Signature. A person who cannot sign his or her name because of illiteracy or a physical disability may make a mark, an "X" for example, as a signature as long as the mark is witnessed by two persons in addition to the Notary. Both witnesses also sign the document (INPH).

Witnesses for Notarization. For a signature by mark to be notarized, there must be two witnesses to the making of the mark in addition to the Notary. Both witnesses must sign the document. The Notary should write out the marker's name beside the mark.

A mark should also be affixed in the Notary's journal, and the witnesses should sign the journal as well.

Notarization Procedures. Because a properly witnessed mark is regarded as a signature by custom and law, the Notary otherwise uses no special procedures. The marker must be positively identified, just like any other signer.

The following certificate is required by the Secretary of State (INPH):

State of Illinois

County of _____

This instrument was acknowledged before me on _____ (date) by _____ (name of person) who made and acknowledged making his/her mark on the instrument in my presence and in the presence of two persons who have signed below.

(Seal)   _____ (Signature of Notary)

_____

Signature and address

of witness

_____

Signature and address

of witness

Notarizing for Minors

Under Age 18. Generally, persons must reach the age of majority before they can handle their own legal affairs and sign documents for themselves. In Illinois, the age of majority is 18. Normally, natural guardians (parents) or court-appointed guardians will sign on a minor's behalf. In certain cases where minors are engaged in a business transaction or serving as court witnesses, they may lawfully sign documents and have their signatures notarized.

Include Age Next to Signature. When notarizing for a minor, the Notary should ask the minor signer to write his or her age next to the signature to alert any person relying on the document that the signer is a minor. The Notary is not required to verify the minor signer's age.

Identification. The method for identifying a minor is the same as that for an adult. However, determining the identity of a minor can be a problem because minors often do not possess acceptable identification documents, such as driver licenses or passports. If the minor does not have acceptable ID, then one of the other methods of identifying signers must be used, either the Notary's personal knowledge of the minor or the oath of a credible identifying witness who can identify the minor. (See "Identifying Document Signers," pages 37–40.)

Foreign Languages

Non-English Advertisements. A nonattorney Notary who advertises notarial services in a language other than English by any form of communication other than a single desk plaque must post with the advertisement the following, in English and in the same language as the advertisement:

"I AM NOT AN ATTORNEY IN ILLINOIS AND MAY NOT GIVE LEGAL ADVICE OR ACCEPT FEES FOR LEGAL ADVICE."

A schedule, written in both languages, of allowed Notary fees must be posted with the announcement.

If the advertisement is by radio or television, the statement may be modified, but must include substantially the same message (5 ILCS 312/3-103).

A Notary may not in any advertisement use the literal translation from English to any language terms or titles including, but not limited to, Notary Public, Notary, licensed, attorney, lawyer or any other term that implies that the person is an attorney (5 ILCS 312/3-103[a]).

Violations of the foreign-language advertisement provisions are punishable by a $1,000 fine for each offense, commission suspension upon the second violation and permanent revocation of the Notary's commission upon the third violation. In addition, the Notary may be subject to other civil or criminal penalties (5 ILCS 312/3-103[a]).

Foreign-Language Documents. Ideally, documents in foreign languages should be referred to an Illinois Notary who reads and writes those languages. If not available, bilingual Notaries often may be found in foreign consulates.

Illinois law does not directly address notarizing documents written in a language the Notary cannot read. Although notarizing such documents is not expressly prohibited, there are difficulties and dangers in notarizing any document the Notary cannot understand. The foremost danger is that the document may have been misrepresented to the Notary. The Notary will not know if the document is false and may unknowingly perform an illegal act by notarizing it.

If a Notary chooses to notarize a document that he or she cannot read, the notarial certificate should be in English or in a language the Notary can read.

Foreign-Language Signers. Illinois statute specifies that if a signer does not speak or understand English, the "nature and effect" of the document must be translated into a language that the person does understand before the document can be notarized (5 ILCS 312/6-104[f]).

The best course of action is to refer the signer to a bilingual Notary, since there should always be direct communication between the Notary and document signer — whether in English or any other language. The Notary should never rely upon an intermediary or interpreter to be assured that a signer is willing, aware and understands the transaction, given that the third party may have a motive for misrepresenting the circumstances to the Notary and/or the signer.

Immigration

Do Not Give Advice. Nonattorney Notaries may never advise others on the subject of immigration, nor help others prepare immigration documents — and especially not for a fee. Notaries who offer immigration advice to others may be prosecuted for the unauthorized practice of law (5 ILCS 312/7-109).

Documents. Affidavits are the forms issued or accepted by the U.S. Citizenship and Immigration Service (USCIS) that most often require notarization, with the Affidavit of Support (I-134) being perhaps the most common. Non-USCIS-issued documents are often notarized and submitted in support of an immigration or naturalization petition. These might include translator's declarations, statements from employers and banks and affidavits of relationship.

If there appears to be no room for the Illinois Notary stamp on an USCIS-issued document, federal officials advise that the seal may be affixed over boilerplate text (standard clauses or sections).

Naturalization Certificates. A Notary may only photocopy a certificate of naturalization for lawful purposes. The National Notary Association recommends that a Notary perform a copy certification by document custodian of the certificate if written directions are provided by a U.S. immigration authority.

Wills

Do Not Offer Advice. Often, people attempt to draw up wills on their own without benefit of legal counsel and then bring these homemade testaments to a Notary to have them "legalized," expecting the Notary to know how to proceed. In advising or assisting such persons, the Notary risks prosecution for the unauthorized practice of law. The Notary's ill-informed advice may do considerable damage to the affairs of the signer and subject the Notary to a civil lawsuit.

Wills are highly sensitive documents, the format of which is strictly dictated by laws. The slightest deviation from these laws can nullify a will. In some cases, holographic (handwritten) wills have actually been voided by notarization because the document was not entirely in the handwriting of the testator.

Do Not Notarize Without Certificate Wording. A Notary should notarize a document described as a will only if a notarial certificate is provided or stipulated for each signer, and the signers are not asking questions about how to proceed. Any such questions should properly be answered by an attorney.

Living Wills. Documents that are popularly called "living wills" may be notarized. These are not actually wills at all, but written statements of the signer's wishes concerning medical treatment in the event that person has an illness or injury and is unable to issue instructions on his or her own behalf.

Notarial Record

Effective June 1, 2009 through June 30, 2013, Illinois Notaries must create a notarial record for every notarization involving a document of conveyance transferring or purporting to transfer title to residential real property located in Cook County (5 ILCS 312/3-102). Note: the new law applies to all Illinois Notaries and not only to those Notaries whose commissions are filed in Cook County.

Background. Senate Bill 546 of 2007 was enacted in response to the growing and vexing problem of real property fraud in Cook County, Illinois.

Notarial Record Is Not a Journal. The notarial record that must be completed for each notarization involving a document of conveyance is not to be confused with the record a Notary makes in a journal of notarial acts. (See "Journal of Notarial Acts," pages 40-43) The journal and notarial record are not one and the same for the following reasons:

- The Notary records a journal entry for all notarial acts, whereas the notarial record is created only for a notarization performed on a document of conveyance transferring or purporting to transfer title to residential real property in Cook County, Illinois.

- The journal record is kept in a bound book or electronic device in chronological order of occurrence, whereas the notarial record is created on a separate sheet of paper or by using electronic means.

- The journal record is kept by the Notary after the completion of a notarial act, whereas the notarial record must be submitted to the Notary's employer or the Cook County Recorder of Deeds.

- Keeping a journal is not required by Illinois law (although strongly recommended), whereas creating a notarial record is required for a notarization performed on a document of conveyance transferring or purporting to transfer title to residential real property in Cook County.

- The journal record kept by the Notary may be inspected by any member of the public, whereas the notarial record containing the thumb- or fingerprint of each signer of a residential real property conveyance document is specifically exempt from inspection and copying under the Freedom of Information Act and may be disclosed only upon receipt of a subpoena issued by a court of competent jurisdiction.

Document of Conveyance. A "document of conveyance" means a written instrument that transfers, or purports to transfer, title effecting a change in ownership of residential real property. Documents of conveyance do not include the following (5 ILCS 312/3-102[b][1]):

- Court-ordered and court-authorized conveyances of residential real property, including quitclaim deeds executed in connection with certain divorce proceedings and transfers in the administration of a probate estate

- Judicial sale deeds that relate to residential real property, including sale deeds in foreclosure proceedings or in execution of a levy to enforce a judgment

- Deeds that transfer ownership of residential real property to a trust when the beneficiary and grantor are the same person

- Deeds that change the nature or type of tenancy on residential real property but that do not transfer ownership from the grantor to another person

- Deeds that establish a tenancy by which both the original grantor and a new person own the residential real property

- Deeds that are executed to the mortgagee in lieu of foreclosure

- Deeds that transfer ownership of residential real property to a trust when the grantor is a beneficiary

Residential Real Property. Under the new law, "residential real property" means a building or buildings containing 1 to 4 units located in Cook County, Illinois, or an individual residential condominium unit. Note: the requirement to create a notarial record for residential real property does not apply to any other county of the state.

Contents of Notarial Record. Each notarial record must contain the following information (5 ILCS 312/3-102[c]):

- The date of the notarial act

- The title, the type or a description of the document of conveyance

- The property index number — a numerical code for the description of a piece of land as it has been defined for the purposes of real estate taxation — (PIN) used to identify the property

- The common street address of the property that is the subject of the document of conveyance

- The signature and printed name and residence street address of each signer (including any agent acting on behalf of a principal under a properly executed power-of-attorney document)

- A certification by each signer that states that "The undersigned grantor hereby certifies that the real property identified in this Notarial Record is Residential Real Property as defined in the Illinois Notary Public Act"

- A description of how the signer was identified (see "Journal Entries," pages 41–42)

- The date of the notarization

- The fee charged for the notarial act

- The Notary's home or business phone number

- The Notary's residence street address

- The Notary's commission expiration date

- The legal name of the Notary's employer

- The business street address of the Notary's employer

- The right thumbprint of the signer or agent acting on behalf of a principal signer under a duly executed power of attorney, or, if the right thumbprint is unavailable, the print of any available finger and an indication of such on the notarial record, or, if the signer or agent is unable to provide a print of any kind, an explanation of the person's physical condition preventing a thumb- or fingerprint from being taken

Electronic Notarial Record. According to the law, a Notary may obtain the thumb- or fingerprint for a notarial record by any means that reliably captures the image, including by electronic means (5 ILCS 312/3-102[c][6]). For example, a Notary could use a computer bioprint scanner as the capturing device. The ability to use electronic means to capture the thumb- or fingerprint implies that the notarial record itself may be electronic.

Furthermore, the law states that "the Notarial Record or other medium containing the thumbprint or fingerprint ... shall be made available or disclosed only upon receipt of a subpoena duly authorized by a court of competent jurisdiction" (5 ILCS 312/3-102[i]), which implies that the notarial record may exist in electronic form. In order for a notarial record to be created electronically, the record must contain all elements required by law, including the signature of the signer.

Disposition of Notarial Record. If a notarial record is created by a Notary who is a principal, employee or agent of a title insurance company, title insurance agent, financial institution or attorney, the Notary must deliver the original notarial record to his or her employer within 14 days of the notarization. The Notary's employer must retain the notarial record for 7 years. (5 ILCS 312/3-102[d]).

If a notarial record is created by a Notary who is not a principal, employee or agent of the aforementioned entities, the Notary must deliver the notarial record, including a $5 filing fee, to the Cook County Recorder of Deeds within 14 days of the notarization (5 ILCS 312/3-102[e]). A notarial record may be submitted to the downtown Chicago, Bridgeview, Markham, Maywood, Rolling Meadows or Skokie office locations.

Retention by Notary Prohibited. Notaries may not retain the original or a copy of an original notarial record (5 ILCS 312/3-102[g])

Form of Notarial Record. The notarial record must be in substantially the following form (5 ILCS 312/3-102[f]):

NOTARIAL RECORD — RESIDENTIAL
REAL PROPERTY TRANSACTIONS

Date Notarized:

Fee: $

The undersigned grantor hereby certifies that the real property identified in this Notarial Record is Residential Real Property as defined in the Illinois Notary Public Act.

Grantor's (Signer's) Printed Name:

Grantor's (Signer's) Signature:

Grantor's (Signer's) Residential Street Address, City, State, and Zip:

Type or Name of Document of Conveyance:

PIN No. of Residential Real Property:

Common Street Address of Residential Real Property:

Thumbprint or Fingerprint:

Description of Means of Identification:

Additional Comments:

Name of Notary Printed:

Notary Phone Number:

Commission Expiration Date:

Residential Street Address of Notary, City, State, and Zip:

Name of Notary's Employer or Principal:

Business Street Address of Notary's Employer or Principal, City, State, and Zip:

Copies of Notarial Records. Notaries may not make or retain copies of an original notarial record. The Notary's employer or principal responsible for retaining the original notarial record may retain copies of the notarial record as part of its business records (5 ILCS 312/3-102[g]).

Failure to Create Notarial Record. A Notary's failure to create a notarial record for a document of conveyance shall not affect the validity of the transaction, in the absence of fraud, but could constitute official misconduct (5 ILCS 312/3-102[h] and 312/7-104).

Disclosure of Notarial Record Prohibited. The law specifically prohibits disclosure of a paper or electronic notarial record under the Freedom of Information Act to any other party, other than a party in succession of interest to the party maintaining the notarial record. For example, a Notary could not allow a member of the public to inspect the notarial record after it was created but before the Notary delivers it to the Notary's employer or Recorder of Deeds of Cook County (5 ILCS 312/3-102[i]).

Military-Officer Notarizations

May Notarize Worldwide. Certain U.S. military officers may notarize for military personnel and their dependents anywhere in the world. Under statutory authority, the following persons are authorized to act as Notaries:

- Civilian attorneys employed as legal assistance attorneys and licensed to practice law in the United States.

- Judge advocates on active duty or training as reservists on inactive duty.

- All adjutants, assistant adjutants, acting adjutants and personnel adjutants.

- Enlisted paralegals, personnel rank E-4 or higher, on active duty or training on inactive duty.

- Active duty personnel who are commissioned officers or senior noncommissioned officers (rank E-7 or higher) who are stationed at a Geographically Separated Unit (GSU) or location where no authorized Notary official is available, and who are appointed in writing by the unit's servicing general court-martial convening authority.

Certificate. When signing documents in their official capacity, military-officer Notaries must specify the date and location of the notarization, their title and office and use a raised seal or inked stamp citing Title 10 U.S.C. 1044a (U.S. Code, Title 10, Sections 936, 1044a).

Authentication. Authentication of a military-officer notarization certificate is not required.

Blank or Incomplete Documents

Do Not Notarize. The Illinois Notary Public Handbook cautions Notaries never to notarize a blank or incomplete document. This is a dangerous, unbusinesslike practice and a breach of common sense, similar to signing a blank check.

A fraudulent document could readily be created above a Notary's signed and sealed certificate on an otherwise blank paper. Additionally, with documents containing blanks to be filled in after the notarization by a person other than the signer, there is a danger that the information inserted will be contrary to the wishes of the signer.

Any blanks in a document should be filled in by the signer. If the blanks are inapplicable and intended to be left unfilled, the signer should be asked to line through each space or write "Not Applicable" or "N/A."

Refusal of Service

Legal Request for Services. Notaries are appointed by the state of Illinois to serve the general public, even when their appointment fee, seal and notarial supplies are paid for by a private employer. A person's race, gender, religion, nationality, ethnicity, lifestyle or political views are never legitimate cause for refusing to perform a notarial act. As a public servant, a Notary should treat all people fairly and equally.

A Notary does have the right to refuse a notarization for due cause (e.g., a suspicious ID). According to state officials, Notaries who refuse to provide services should be cautioned of potential discrimination lawsuits for refusing to notarize without reason. Such reason and any other pertinent information regarding the refusal should be noted in the Notary's journal.

Business Hours. Notaries are not expected to be available to notarize for the public other than during the Notary's normal business hours. However, a Notary may elect to offer notarial services at any hour.

Reasonable Care

Responsibility. As public servants, Notaries must act responsibly and exercise reasonable care in the performance of their official duties. If a Notary fails to do so, he or she may be subject to a civil suit to recover financial damages caused by the Notary's error.

In general, reasonable care is the degree of attentiveness that a person of normal intelligence and responsibility would exhibit. If a Notary can show a judge or jury that he or she did everything expected of a reasonable person, the judge or jury is obligated by law to find the Notary not liable for damages.

Complying with all pertinent laws is the first rule of

61

reasonable care for a Notary. If there are no statutory guidelines in a given instance, the Notary should go to extremes to use common sense and prudence. (See "Steps to Proper Notarization," pages 14-18.)

Authentication

Documents Sent Out of State. Documents notarized in Illinois and sent out of state may be required to bear proof that the Notary's signature and stamp are genuine and that the Notary had authority to act at the time of notarization. This process of proving the genuineness of an official signature and seal is called authentication or legalization.

Locally, an authenticating certificate for an Illinois Notary may be obtained at the office of the county clerk where the Notary's appointment has been recorded. The county clerk keeps a record of the Notary's appointment and of the time the appointment expires.

Authenticating certificates for Notaries, including apostilles, are also issued by the Illinois Secretary of State's office (5 ILCS 312/3-106).

Authenticating certificates are known by many different names: certificates of official character, certificates of authority, certificates of capacity, certificates of prothonotary and "flags."

Anyone who requires a certificate of authority should contact the county clerk or the Secretary of State's Index Department. It is not the responsibility of the Notary Public to obtain authentication.

The fee for a certificate of authority, including an apostille, is $2. Authentication may be obtained by mail or in person from:

Department of Index
111 East Monroe Street
Springfield, IL 62756
(217) 558-2972

For notarized documents sent from Illinois to other U.S. states and jurisdictions, a single certificate of authority from the county clerk or Illinois Secretary of State is normally sufficient authentication.

Documents Sent Out of the Country. If the notarized document is going outside the United States, a chain authentication process may be necessary, and additional certificates of authority may have to be obtained from the U.S. Department of State in Washington, a foreign consulate in Washington and a ministry of foreign affairs in the particular foreign nation.

Apostilles and the Hague Convention. More than 90 nations, including the United States, subscribe to a treaty under auspices of the Hague Conference that simplifies authentication of notarized documents exchanged between these nations. The official name of this treaty, adopted by the Conference on October 5, 1961, is the *Hague Convention Abolishing the Requirement of Legalization for Foreign Public Documents.* (For a list of the subscribing countries, see "Hague Convention Nations," pages 125–127.)

Under the Hague Convention, only one authenticating certificate called an *apostille* is necessary to ensure acceptance in these subscribing countries. (*Apostille* is French for "notation.")

In Illinois, *apostilles* are also issued by the Secretary of State for a fee of $2 (5 ILCS 312/3-106).

Electronic Notarization

Electronic commerce produces a need for Notaries to witness electronic transactions, just as Notaries have witnessed paper transactions for centuries. While the tools for creating and signing documents may be different, the impartial witnessing services of a Notary remain the same and are as important as ever.

Legislative Background. Effective June 14, 2001, Illinois adopted the Electronic Commerce Security Act, which gives electronic signatures the same legal effect as a hand-rendered signature.

Effective August 27, 2007, Illinois enacted the Uniform Real Property Electronic Recording Act (URPERA). The Act permits a county recorder to establish an electronic recording system for the filing of electronic real property documents executed and notarized with electronic signatures. An electronic notarization performed under the Act is legal without the imprint of the Notary's official physical seal.

Image of Seal Not Required. Section 3 of the URPERA states that an image of an official Notary seal is not required to be included in an electronic notarization as long as all information required to be included in a notarial act by law is attached to or logically associated with the Notary's electronic signature or the electronic real property document. For example, the Notary could satisfy the statute by typing the information included within the Notary's official physical seal near the Notary's electronic signature (765 ILCS 33/3[c]).

MISCONDUCT, FINES AND PENALTIES

Prohibited Acts

Misconduct Defined. Official misconduct means the unauthorized, unlawful, abusive, negligent, reckless or injurious performance of Notary duties (5 ILCS 312/7-104).

Certify Copies. Illinois Notaries are not authorized to certify copies of any documents (INPH).

Blank Spaces. A Notary may not notarize any blank or incomplete document (INPH). Also, a Notary may not sign a blank affidavit or acknowledgment certificate and deliver the signed form for use by another person (5 ILCS 312/6-104[c]).

Declared Incapacity. A Notary may not notarize the signature of a person he or she knows to have been declared mentally ill by a court unless the person has been subsequently restored to mental health as a matter of record (5 ILCS 312/6-104[d]).

Blind Signers. An Illinois Notary is prohibited from taking the acknowledgment of a person who is blind unless the Notary has first read the document to the person (5 ILCS 312/6-104[e]).

Non-English Speaking Signers. Illinois law specifically prohibits Notaries from taking the acknowledgment of anyone who does not speak or understand English unless the nature and effect of the document to be notarized is translated into a language the person does understand (5 ILCS 312/6-104[f]).

Change Documents. Notaries are not allowed to change anything in a document after it has been signed (5 ILCS 312/6-104[g]).

Prepare Documents. Non-attorney Notaries may not assist anyone in preparing a document, nor fill in the blanks on a document, other than the notarial certificate (5 ILCS 312/6-104[h]).

Unauthorized Practice of Law. Non-attorney Notaries may not render, offer to render or hold himself or herself out as rendering any service constituting the unauthorized practice of law (5 ILCS 312/7-109).

Advertising. An Illinois Notary may not literally translate from English into another language terms or titles including, but not limited to, "Notary Public," "Notary," "licensed," "attorney," "lawyer" or any other term that implies that he or she is an attorney. Further, a Notary may not advertise in a language other than English, without posting a disclaimer in English and the foreign language stating that the Notary is not an attorney and may not give or charge for legal advice (5 ILCS 312/3-103[a] and 3-103[b]).

Immigration Expert. A nonattorney Notary may not represent himself or herself to be an immigration expert unless he or she is designated by the U.S. Citizenship and Immigration Service or by the Board of Immigration Appeals (5 ILCS 312/3-103[c]).

Fail to Transmit Funds. Notaries must transmit or forward funds that they have taken from a person for whom they have performed a notarization and that they have accepted specifically for the purpose of transmitting or forwarding to another person (5 ILCS 312/6-104[i]).

Make or Retain Copies of Notarial Record. Notaries may not make or retain copies of an original notarial record (5 ILCS 312/3-102[g]).

Disclosure of Notarial Record. Notaries may not allow any person other than a party in succession of interest to the party maintaining a notarial record to inspect the notarial record (5 ILCS 312/3-102[i]).

Failure to Create Notarial Record. A negligent failure to create a notarial record for a document of conveyance affecting or purporting to affect title to residential real property in Cook County, Illinois, from June 1, 2009, through June 30, 2013, could constitute official misconduct as defined in the Notary

Public Act. A failure to create a notarial record shall not affect the validity of the residential real property transaction, in the absence of fraud (5 ILCS 312/3-102[h]).

Failure to Keep Records and Provide Receipts for Fees. A Notary's failure to keep records and provide receipts for fees accepted for notarial services could constitute official misconduct as defined in the Notary Public Act. In addition, a failure to keep records and provide receipts that can be presented as evidence of no wrongdoing shall be construed as presumptive admission of allegations raised in complaints against the Notary for violations related to accepting prohibited fees (5 ILCS 312/6-104[d]).

Refusal or Revocation of Appointment

Application Misstatement or Omission. The Illinois Secretary of State will deny or revoke the appointment of any Notary or applicant who submits an application containing any substantial and material misstatement or omission of fact (5 ILCS 312/7-108[a]).

Felony or Official Misconduct. The Secretary of State will deny or revoke the appointment of any Notary or applicant found guilty of any felony or official misconduct (5 ILCS 312/7-108[b]).

Previous Revocation. Previous revocation of an Illinois Notary appointment within a 10-year period is cause for denial of a new appointment by the Secretary of State (5 ILCS 312/2-102).

Civil Lawsuit

Liability of Notary. As a ministerial official, an Illinois Notary is liable for all damages caused by any intentional or unintentional misconduct or neglect. The $5,000 bond offers no protection to the Notary since the Notary is required by law to reimburse the bonding firm for any funds paid out to a victim of the Notary's misconduct. A civil lawsuit against the Notary may seek financial recovery against any and all of the Notary's personal assets (5 ILCS 312/7-101).

Liability of Employer. The employer of a Notary may also be held liable for damages proximately caused by a Notary acting within the scope of his or her employment and whose notarial actions are known and permitted by the employer (5 ILCS 312/7-102).

Criminal Penalties

Official Misconduct. A Notary who knowingly and willfully commits any official misconduct is guilty of a Class A Misdemeanor (5 ILCS 312/7-105).

A Notary who negligently commits any official misconduct is guilty of a Class B Misdemeanor (5 ILCS 312/7-105).

Willful Impersonation. A person who impersonates a Notary while not lawfully commissioned is guilty of a Class A Misdemeanor (5 ILCS 312/7-106).

Wrongful Possession. A person who unlawfully possesses a Notary's official seal is guilty of a misdemeanor and subject to a fine not exceeding $1,000 (5 ILCS 312/7-107). ■

Test Your Knowledge

Self Exam

Instructions. This examination is designed to test your knowledge of the basic concepts of notarization.

Work through the exam without looking at the answers, then check your responses and note where you need additional study. Careful review of "Notary Laws Explained" (pages 19–67), the reprinted Notary rules and statutes (pages 74–112), "10 Most-Asked Questions" (pages 9–13) and "Steps to Proper Notarization" (pages 14–18) will produce the answers.

A perfect score on this examination is 100 points. There are:

- Twenty true/false questions worth one point each.

- Five multiple-choice questions worth four points each.

- Five fill-in-the-blank questions worth four points each.

- Five essay questions worth eight points each.

Now, get a separate sheet of paper and a pen or pencil, and get ready to test your knowledge.

True/False. For the following statements, answer true or false. Each correct answer is worth one point:

1. Notaries may act only in the county where they are appointed and reside. True or false?

2. The maximum Notary fee for taking the acknowledgment of three signers is $6. True or false?

3. It is a Notary's duty to serve all persons requesting lawful notarial acts, even those who are not customers. True or false?

4. Notaries must keep a photocopy of every document notarized. True or false?

5. An Illinois Notary is authorized to notarize a jurat attached to a deposition. True or false?

6. Notaries can withhold their services if they believe a signer is unable to understand a document.
True or false?

7. The best Notary journal is one with replaceable loose-leaf pages. True or false?

8. The letters "L.S." stand for the Latin words *locus sigilli*, which mean "location of the seal." True or false?

9. Holographic wills must be notarized to be valid. True or false?

10. A credible witness vouches for the identity of a signer in the Notary's presence. True or false?

11. A Notary may notarize other signatures on a document co-signed by the Notary. True or false?

12. A signer who is unable to write can sign by mark if the mark is witnessed by two other persons in addition to the Notary. True or false?

13. The Notary need not reimburse the surety company for bond funds paid out to a person financially harmed by the Notary's actions. True or false?

14. After the letters "S.S.," the Notary must write his or her Social Security number. True or false?

15. A Notary's stamp and journal belong to the Notary's employer only if the employer paid for them. True or false?

16. An acknowledgment certificate is not to be used for jurats. True or false?

17. An affirmation is the legal equivalent of an oath, but has no reference to a Supreme Being. True or false?

18. An Illinois Notary employed by a private employer may charge an additional fee for a notarization that requires an excessive amount of time. True or false?

19. The Notary can make necessary corrections to a document after signing, if the corrections are properly initialed and dated. True or false?

20. A newly-commissioned Notary has 90 days from the time he or she is notified to record the appointment as a Notary with the county clerk. True or false?

Multiple Choice. Choose the one best answer to each question. Each correct answer is worth four points.

1. A Notary has no disqualifying interest when acting as ...
    a. A cosigner of the document.
    b. An owner of the company involved in the transaction.
    c. A salaried employee of the signer's company.

2. To become a Notary, an applicant must ...
    a. Have been a state resident for at least one year.
    b. File a bond and take an oath.
    c. Pass an oral exam given by the Governor's office.

3. A certificate of authority for a Notary may be obtained ...
    a. Only from the office of the county clerk.
    b. From the office of the county clerk or the Illinois Secretary of State.
    c. Only from the office of the Illinois Governor.

4. "Satisfactory evidence" of identity means reliance ...
    a. On IDs, a credible witness or personal knowledge.

    b. Only on ID cards or personal knowledge of identity.

    c. Only on a credible witness or personal knowledge.

5. An Illinois Notary may ...

    a. Notarize a certification by a document custodian.

    b. Certify copies of computer software.

    c. Certify a copy of a foreign birth certificate.

Fill in the Blank. Write in the word or phrase that best completes each sentence. Each correct answer is worth four points.

1. The Notary and the _____ for the Notary's bond are liable for the Notary's neglect and misconduct.

2. A solemn, spoken pledge that is not an affirmation is called a(n) _____.

3. The most reliable type of ID card contains a signature and a(n) _____ of its bearer.

4. Without ID cards or personal knowledge of a signer's identity, Notaries may rely upon the oath of a(n) _____ to identify the stranger.

5. Wills written entirely in the testator's own handwriting are called _____.

Essay. Reply to each question or statement with a short paragraph. Each complete and correct response is worth eight points.

1. Discuss the distinctions between a Notary bond and Notary errors and omissions insurance.

2. Why is a Social Security card not an acceptable form of ID?

3. What is an *apostille* and when is it used?

4. Why should a Notary always complete the journal entry before filling out a notarial certificate?

5. Outline the differences between an acknowledgment certificate and a jurat.

Test Answers

True/False. 1. F; 2. F; 3. T; 4. F; 5. T; 6. T; 7. F; 8. T; 9. F; 10. T; 11. F; 12. T; 13. F; 14. F; 15. F; 16. T; 17. T; 18. F; 19. F; 20. F

Multiple Choice. 1. c; 2. b; 3. b; 4. a; 5. a

Fill In The Blank. 1. Surety; 2. Oath; 3. Photograph; 4. Credible witness; 5. Holographic

Essay. Responses should include the basic information in the paragraphs below:

1. A Notary bond, obtained through a state-licensed surety company, provides protection for the public in case of the Notary's negligence or intentional misconduct. Up to the cash limit of the bond, the surety agrees to pay damages to anyone who suffers a loss because of the Notary's actions; the Notary, however, must then reimburse the surety. Notary errors and omissions insurance, also purchased from a state-licensed company, protects the Notary in case of an unintentional error, up to the policy limit. The Notary does not reimburse the insurance company. A bond is required by law; errors and omissions insurance is not.

2. A Social Security card is very easily counterfeited and has only one of the elements of an acceptable ID, a signature. Acceptable IDs also must bear a photograph.

3. An *apostille* is a certificate authenticating the signature and seal of a Notary that is issued under provisions of an international treaty, signed by more than 90 nations, called the *Hague Convention Abolishing the Requirement of Legalization for Foreign Public Documents*. For notarized documents exchanged between the subscribing nations, this treaty streamlines the time-consuming authentication process known as "chain certification" by requiring only one authenticating certificate, the *apostille* (French for "notation"). *Apostilles* for Illinois Notaries are issued by the Secretary of State in Springfield.

4. Filling out a journal entry before completing a notarial certificate prevents a signer from leaving with the document before an important record of the notarization is made in the journal.

5. An acknowledgment certificate certifies that the signer of the document personally appeared before the Notary on the date and in the county indicated. It also certifies that the signer's identity was satisfactorily proven to the Notary and that the signer acknowledged having signed freely. A jurat certifies that the person signing the document did so in the Notary's presence, the person appeared before the Notary on the date and in the county indicated, the signer's identity was satisfactorily proven to the Notary and the Notary administered an oath or affirmation to the signer.

Tally Your Score

After checking your answers, add up your score. Then look at the grading scale below to determine how you stand:

- 90–100: Excellent!

- 80–89: Good, but some review needed.

- 70–79: Fair. Reread the parts of the *Primer* covering the answers you missed.

- Below 70: Below par. Study the laws thoroughly again. ■

Illinois Laws Pertaining to Notaries Public

The pertinent sections of the most recently published Illinois Notary Public Handbook (INPH), issued to newly appointed Notaries by the Secretary of State, and Illinois statutes are reprinted on the following pages.

This official booklet contains pertinent sections of the Illinois Notary Public Act (INPA) that govern Notaries and notarial acts. It also contains helpful instructions on notarial matters not addressed in the statutes.

ILLINOIS NOTARY HANDBOOK

Secretary of State
Index Department
111 E. Monroe Street
Springfield, Illinois 62756

A Message From Secretary of State Jesse White

Dear Friend:

This handbook outlines the important duties of a notary public. The Illinois Notary Public Act, effective July 1, 1986, was passed to better meet the needs of the modern business world. Effective June 13, 2000, under certain conditions, residents of states bordering Illinois may be commissioned as Illinois notaries.

Following are basic rules for proper and safe notarization: 1) Keep your notary seal in a safe place; 2) Do not notarize a signature unless the signer is present at the time of notarization; 3) Do not lend your stamp to anyone, including your employer; 4) Do not identify a document signer on the word of a friend or employer who is not willing to take an oath; 5) Sign your name on notarial certificates exactly as it appears on your commission and affix your seal.

I encourage you to read this handbook thoroughly. If you have questions please contact: Office of the Secretary of State, Index Department, 111 E. Monroe Street, Springfield, IL 62756.

Sincerely,
Jesse White
Secretary of State

General Information*

Introduction

An Illinois notary public holds an important office and must fully understand the functions and responsibilities of that office as set forth by Illinois law. Effective June 13, 2000, under certain conditions, residents of states bordering Illinois may be commissioned as Illinois notaries.

The purpose of notarization is to prevent fraud and forgery. The notary acts as an official and unbiased witness to the identity of a person who comes before the notary for a specific purpose. This places a great deal of responsibility upon the notary.

If a document requires the administration of an oath, the person must personally appear before the notary, be administered the appropriate oath, and sign the document in the notary's presence.

If the document requires an acknowledgment, the person must appear before the notary and acknowledge the document.

Following is a summary of general information relating to notaries. Section numbers appearing in the text refer to sections of the Illinois Notary Public Act, which is printed in its entirety beginning on page 83.

Appointment

Illinois residents are appointed notaries by the Secretary of State for a term of four years. Out-of-state residents are appointed for a one-year term. An applicant for appointment must: (1) be a citizen of the United States or an alien lawfully admitted for permanent residence; (2) be a resident of the State of Illinois or employed in the state of Illinois for at least 30 days; (3) be at least 18 years of age; (4) be able to read and write the English language; (5) have not been convicted of a felony; and (6) have not had a notary commission revoked during the past 10 years (Sec. 2-102).

An applicant must complete the proper application form provided by

---

*Although every effort has been made to ensure the accuracy of this information, it is not intended as a substitute for the law or for opinions and decisions of the courts.

the Secretary of State, which includes the oath of office. He or she must also obtain from a bonding or surety company a $5,000 notary bond. The application and bond are then forwarded to the Secretary of State along with the $10 filing fee. If the Secretary of State approves the application, a commission will be issued.

The commission will be mailed to the county clerk of the county in which the applicant resides. The appointment is not complete until the commission is recorded with the county clerk. The recording with the county clerk may be done in person or by mail. The county clerk will notify the applicant of the procedure (Sec. 2-106).

When the applicant has recorded his or her appointment with the county clerk and has received the commission, the appointment is complete. The notary must then obtain an official seal and can perform notarial acts anywhere in the State of Illinois, as long as he or she continues to reside or work in the county in which he or she was commissioned.

Bond

The $5,000 bond must be issued by a company qualified to write surety bonds in the State of Illinois (Sec. 2-105). In order for a company to write bonds, that company must be qualified to do so with the Illinois Department of Insurance. Although the company you work for may be willing to post a bond for you, it probably is not qualified to do so.

Most insurance companies can write surety bonds. You may want to contact your local agent. The decision where to purchase a bond can only be made by the applicant. The Office of the Secretary of State does not recommend any particular bonding company.

Seal

Every notary public must obtain and use a rubber stamp seal no more than one inch in height and two and one-half inches in length (Sec. 3-101). Although the law does not prescribe the exact format of the seal, the following example contains all of the required information and is acceptable. In this case, the notary's name is John Doe, whose notary appointment expires December 31, 2007.

OFFICIAL SEAL
JOHN H. DOE
NOTARY PUBLIC, STATE OF ILLINOIS
My Commission Expires 12-31-07

(seal must be in black ink)

The stamp must include the notary public's name exactly as the notary was commissioned and the date upon which the notary's commission expires. (This date appears on the notary commission.) You may include the name of the county in which your appointment is recorded on your seal. The law neither requires the name of the county to appear on the seal nor prohibits it.

Notary seals may be purchased at most office supply stores or stamp manufacturers. Consult the yellow pages of your telephone book for "rubber stamps." The Office of the Secretary of State does not recommend any particular company.

Failure to Record Appointment with County Clerk

If the applicant fails to record his or her appointment with the county clerk within 60 days, the county clerk will return the commission to the Secretary of State, and the commission will be cancelled. No refund will be issued (Sec. 2-106).

Signature

A notary public must sign every notary certificate and affix the seal at the time of notarization. A notary shall not use any name or initial in signing certificates other than that by which the notary was commissioned (Sec. 6-104). If you are commissioned as a notary JOHN DOE, you must sign notary certificates JOHN DOE. You cannot sign JOHN A. DOE or JOHNNY DOE. Make sure your name on the application reads the way you intend to sign your name.

Geographical Jurisdiction

A notary public has jurisdiction to act as such throughout the state of Illinois (Sec. 3-105). In the certificates a notary is called upon to complete, there will be a heading such as "State of Illinois, County of _____." The name of the county where the signer personally appeared before the notary public should be inserted on the certificate.

Fee

The maximum fee that may be charged by a notary for a notarial act is $1. A notary is not required to charge for services.

Certificate of Authority

Courts or public officials may require that a "Certificate of Authority" be attached to a document that has been notarized. This certificate confirms that the individual was an appointed and commissioned notary public for the State of Illinois on the date of notarization. Such certificates are issued by the county clerk of the county where the notary recorded his or her appointment or by the Secretary of State. Persons who require a certificate of authority should contact the county clerk or the Secretary of State's Index Department for further information. Most documents do not require a certificate of authority, and it is not the responsibility of the notary public to obtain such a certificate for any party.

Change of Name or Move to Another County

The law requires a notary public to resign his or her appointment if there is a change in name, a move to another county, or non-resident notary changes employment to another county (Sec. 4-101). If the person wishes to continue to be a notary, he or she must apply for appointment under the new name or in the new county of residence or employment. This action is necessary so that county clerks can certify the authority of notaries in their counties.

Reappointment as a Notary

Illinois notaries are appointed for either a four-year term or a one-year term. Notaries are not automatically reappointed (Sec. 5-101). A notary public whose appointment is about to expire and who wishes to continue to be a notary shall follow the same procedure used for a new appointment. The Secretary of State sends out renewal notices prior to the expiration date of the current appointment.

Refusal or Revocation of Appointment

The Secretary of State may refuse to appoint any person as a notary public or may revoke the appointment of any notary public upon the following: (a) If an application contains misstatements or omissions of facts; or (b) if a notary public is convicted of any felony or of official misconduct under this Act (Sec. 7-108). A person whose notary public appointment has been revoked may not apply for another appointment during the 10-year period following the revocation.

Functions of a Notary Public

NOTARIAL ACTS — An Illinois notary public is authorized to perform notarial acts or "notarization" anywhere in the state. Notarial acts include taking an acknowledgment, taking a verification upon oath or affirmation, witnessing or attesting a signature, administering an oath or affirmation, and performing any other act authorized by law (Sec. 6-101).

IDENTIFICATION — A notary public must positively identify the person requesting notarization. A notary has positive identification if the person (a) is personally known to the notary; (b) is identified upon the oath or affirmation of a credible witness personally known to the notary; or (c) is identified on the basis of identification documents (Sec. 6-102).

CERTIFICATES — There is a certificate for each type of notarial act. Most documents have a preprinted certificate on the form, or a certificate has been prepared by an attorney. It is not the notary's function to determine what type of notarial act is required with regard to a request, but the notary must know and use the proper certificate for the type of act he or she is requested to perform (Sec. 6-103). A brief description of each type of notarial act and the related certificate follows.

Acknowledgment

The taking of an acknowledgment consists of positively identifying the signer of a document. The signer need not sign in the notary's presence but must personally appear before the notary and state that the signature on the document is his or hers. Acknowledgments may be taken in an individual capacity or in a representative capacity (as an authorized representative of another — for example, as officer of a corporation for and on behalf of the corporation or as an attorney in fact for another person). These short form certificates are sufficient to meet the requirements of the law.

Acknowledgment
(in an individual capacity)

State of Illinois

County of _____

This instrument was acknowledged before me on _____ (date) by _____ (name of person).

(seal)   _____ (signature of notary public)

Acknowledgment
(in a representative capacity)

State of Illinois

County of _____

This instrument was acknowledged before me on _____ (date) by _____ (name of person) as _____ (type of authority, e.g., officer, trustee, etc.) of _____ (name of party on behalf of whom instrument was executed).

(seal) _____ (signature of notary public)

Verification Upon Oath or Affirmation

Sometimes referred to as a "jurat," verification upon oath or affirmation is a declaration that a statement is true and was made by a person upon oath or affirmation. The person requesting this notarial act must personally appear before the notary and sign the document in the presence of the notary. The notary public is required to administer an oath. There is no prescribed wording for the oath, but an acceptable oath would be:

"DO YOU SWEAR (OR AFFIRM) THAT THE STATEMENTS IN THIS DOCUMENT ARE TRUE?"

Verification upon oath may be taken in an individual capacity or in a representative capacity. These short form certificates are sufficient to meet the requirements of the law.

Verification upon Oath or Affirmation

(in an individual capacity)

State of Illinois

County of _____

Signed and sworn (or affirmed) to before me on _____ (date) by
_____ (name of person making statement).

(seal) _____ (signature of notary public)

Verification upon Oath or Affirmation

(in a representative capacity)

State of Illinois

County of _____

Signed and sworn (or affirmed) to before me on _____ (date) by
_____ (name of person) as _____ (type of authority, e.g., officer,
trustee, etc.) of _____ (name of party on behalf of whom instrument
was executed).

(seal) _____ (signature of notary public)

Witnessing or Attesting a Signature

Occasionally, a notary public may be requested to witness a signature
on a document when no oath is necessary or required. The person
requesting this notarial act must personally appear before the notary and
sign the document in the presence of the notary. This short form certificate
is sufficient to meet the requirements of the law.

Witnessing or Attesting a Signature

State of Illinois

County of _____

Signed (or subscribed or attested) before me on _____ (date) by
_____ (name of person).

(seal) _____ (signature of notary public)

Signature-By-Mark

When an individual requests a notarial act and the individual is prevented by disability or illiteracy from writing a signature. Take these precautions: positively identify the individual; ensure that there are two persons to witness the signature-by-mark in addition to yourself; write in the name of the signer-by-mark near the mark on the document, and complete the form below.

Signature-By-Mark

State of Illinois

County of _____

This instrument was acknowledged before me on _____ (date) by _____ (name of person) who made and acknowledged making his/her mark on the instrument in the presence of two persons who have signed below.

(seal) _____ (signature of notary public)

_____   _____

signature and address   signature and address

of witness   of witness

Oaths or Affirmations

On rare occasions, a notary may be asked to administer a verbal oath or affirmation. Illinois notaries public are authorized to administer such oaths not only by the Notary Public Act but also by other state laws (Illinois Revised Statutes, ch. 101). Notaries may administer oaths to witnesses, the oath of office to public officials when an oath of office is required to be taken, and oaths on any other occasion when an oath is required.

An oath contains the words "I do solemnly swear...," and an affirmation contains the words "I do solemnly affirm... ." Either form may be used, as both are effective in invoking the perjury statute against the maker of a false statement.

The exact wording of the oaths or affirmations can vary from situation to situation. It is not the obligation of a notary to ascertain the proper wording of an oath or affirmation, but the notary can administer it when the proper wording is provided. Following is a constitutional oath or affirmation required to be taken by most elected state and local officials.

Oath or Affirmation

"I do solemnly swear (affirm) that I will support the Constitution of the United States, and the Constitution of the State of Illinois, and that I will faithfully discharge the duties of the office of _____ to the best of my ability."

Prohibited Acts

The law expressly prohibits a notary from performing certain acts set forth in (Sec. 6-104). Notaries are urged to read carefully that section of the law. Notaries are reminded in particular that:

A Notary Public Is Not a Notario Publico

In Mexico and other Spanish-speaking countries, a Notario Publico is a trained attorney with special expertise. A Mexican "notario" can, therefore, give legal advice and prepare legal forms. An Illinois notary does not have this authority. In fact, Illinois notaries who are not attorneys and who advertise notarial services in a language other than English must post a notice in English and the language in which the advertisement appears which states: "I AM NOT AN ATTORNEY LICENSED TO PRACTICE LAW IN ILLINOIS AND MAY NOT GIVE LEGAL ADVICE OR ACCEPT FEES FOR LEGAL ADVICE." If an Illinois notary is approached for help with a legal matter, the notary should refer the person to an attorney.

Immigration Forms

Federal law and regulation allows only attorneys and those persons who are "designated entities" by the United States Citizenship and Immigration Service (USCIS) or Board of Immigration Appeals to assist aliens in the preparation of legalization status. An Illinois notary cannot give advice on immigration matters, complete forms, or charge fees unless he or she has been authorized to do so by the USCIS or is an attorney.

A Notary May Not Issue Certified Copies

Illinois law does not authorize a notary public to certify copies of any document. Persons requesting certified copies of documents should be referred to the official who has custody of the original document or to the office where the document has been officially filed.

Penalties and Liability

A notary is held personally liable for all damages caused by his or her official misconduct (Sec. 7-101). "Official misconduct" means the unauthorized, unlawful, abusive, negligent, reckless or injurious performance of a duty. The notary bond does not protect the notary against such liability. The bond gives protection only to the person who is damaged by the notary's misconduct. The bonding company will then recover its loss from the notary. The notary's employer may also be liable for damages, if the notary was acting within the scope of the notary's employment at the time the notary engaged in the official misconduct (Sec. 7-102). In addition to being liable for damages, a notary convicted of official misconduct faces a fine and possible imprisonment.

Conclusion

A notary should act with caution. Questions should be answered by referring to the law or by contacting the Office of the Secretary of State. A notary public should always remember to:

1. Identify the person requesting a notarial act.

2. Administer an oath, if necessary.

3. Carefully complete the notarial certificate.

4. Sign his or her name as it appears on the notary seal.

5. Affix the notary seal.

6. The expiration date of his or her commission must be legible within the seal. No alterations are allowed.

Be sure to read the Act and keep it with your notary seal for later reference.

ILLINOIS NOTARY PUBLIC ACT
(As amended by Public Act 95-988, effective June 1, 2009)
(Illinois Revised Statutes Ch. 102, par. 201-101)
(Illinois Compiled Statutes 5 ILCS 312)

ARTICLE I

General Provisions

1-101. Short Title.
This Act shall be known and may be cited as the "Illinois Notary Public Act" amended by P.A. 86-1475, effective Jan. 10, 1991.

1-102. Purposes and Rules of Construction.
(a) This Act shall be construed and applied to promote its underlying purposes and policies.

(b) The underlying purposes and policies of this Act are:

(1) to simplify, clarify, and modernize the law governing notaries public; and

(2) to promote, serve, and protect the public interest.

1-103. Prospective Effect of Act.
This Act applies prospective. Nothing in this Act shall be construed to revoke any notary public commissions existing on the effective date of this Act. All reappointments of notarial commissions shall be obtained in accordance with this Act.

1-104. Notary Public and Notarization Defined.
(a) The terms "notary public" and "notary" are used interchangeably to mean any individual appointed and commissioned to perform notarial acts.

(b) "Notarization" means the performance of a notarial act.

(c) "Accredited immigration representative" means a not-for-profit organization recognized by the Board of Immigration Appeals under 8 C.F.R.

292.2(a) and employees of those organizations accredited under 8 C.F.R. 292.2(d). (As amended by public act 93-1001, effective August 23, 2004)

ARTICLE II

Appointment Provisions

2-101. Appointment.

The Secretary of State may appoint and commission as notaries public for a four-year term as many persons resident in a county in this State as he deems necessary. The Secretary of State may appoint and commission as notaries public for a one-year term as many persons who are residents of a state bordering Illinois whose place of work or business is within a county in this State as the Secretary deems necessary, but only if laws of that state authorize residents of Illinois to be appointed and commissioned as notaries public in that state.

2-102. Application.

Every applicant for appointment and commission as a notary shall complete an application form furnished by the Secretary of State to be filed with the Secretary of State stating:

(a) the applicant's official name, which contains his or her last name and at least the initial of the first name;

(b) the county in which the applicant resides or, if the applicant is a resident of a state bordering Illinois, the county in Illinois in which that person's principal place of work or principal place of business is located;

(c) the applicant's residence address and business address, if any, or any address at which an applicant will use a notary public commission to receive fees;

(d) that the applicant has resided in the State of Illinois for 30 days preceding the application or that the applicant who is a resident of a state bordering Illinois has worked or maintained a business in Illinois for 30 days preceding the application;

(e) that the applicant is a citizen of the United States or an alien lawfully admitted for permanent residence in the United States;

(f) that the applicant is at least 18 years of age;

(g) that the applicant is able to read and write the English language;

(h) that the applicant has never been the holder of a notary public appointment that was revoked or suspended during the past 10 years;

(i) that the applicant has not been convicted of a felony; and

(j) any other information the Secretary of State deems necessary

(As amended by Public Act 93-1001, effective August 23, 2004).

2-103. Appointment Fee.

Every applicant for appointment and commission as a notary public shall pay to the Secretary of State a fee of $10.

2-104. Oath.

Every applicant for appointment and commission as a notary public shall take the following oath in the presence of a person qualified to administer an oath in this State:

"I, _____ (name of applicant), solemnly affirm, under penalty of perjury, that the answers to all questions in this application are true, complete, and correct; that I have carefully read the notary law of this State; and that, if appointed and commissioned as a notary public, I will perform faithfully, to the best of my ability, all notarial acts in accordance with the law.

_____ (Signature of applicant)

Subscribed and affirmed before me on _____, _____.

(Official signature and official seal of notary)".

(As amended by Public Act 85-1396, effective September 2, 1988.)

2-105. Bond.

Every application for appointment and commission as a notary public shall be accompanied by an executed bond commencing on the date of the appointment with a term of 4 years, in the sum of $5,000, with, as surety thereon, a company qualified to write surety bonds in this State. The bond shall be conditioned upon the faithful performance of all notarial acts in accordance with this Act. The Secretary of State may prescribe an official bond form.

2-106. Appointment Recorded by County Clerk.

The appointment of the applicant as a notary public is complete when the commission is recorded with the county clerk.

The Secretary of State shall forward the applicant's commission to the county clerk of the county in which the applicant resides or, if the applicant is a resident of a state bordering Illinois, the county in Illinois in which the applicant's principal place of work or principal place of business is located. Upon receipt thereof, the county clerk shall notify the applicant of the action taken by the Secretary of State, and the applicant shall either appear at the county clerk's office to record the same and receive the commission or request by mail to have the commission sent to the applicant with a specimen signature of the applicant attached to the request. The applicant shall have a record of the appointment, and the time when the commission will expire, entered in the records of the office of the county clerk. When the applicant appears before the county clerk, the applicant shall pay a fee of $5, at which time the county clerk shall then deliver the commission to the applicant.

If the appointment is completed by mail, the applicant shall pay the county clerk a fee of $10, which shall be submitted with the request to the county clerk. The county clerk shall than record the appointment and send the commission by mail to the applicant.

If an applicant does not respond to the notification by the county clerk within 30 days, the county clerk shall again notify the applicant that the county clerk has received the applicant's notary public commission issued by the Secretary of State. The second notice shall be in substantially the following form:

"The records of this office indicate that you have not picked up your notary public commission from the Office of the County Clerk.

The Illinois Notary Public Law requires you to appear in person in the clerk's office, record your commission, and pay a fee of $5 to the county clerk or request that your commission be mailed to you. This request must be accompanied by a specimen of your signature and $10 fee payable to the county clerk.

Your appointment as a notary is not complete until the commission is recorded with the county clerk. Furthermore, if you do not make arrangements with the clerk for recording and delivery of your commission within 30 days from the date of this letter, the county clerk will return your commission to the Secretary of State. Your commission will be cancelled and your name will be removed from the list of notaries in the State of Illinois.

I should also like to remind you that any person who attests to any document as a notary and is not a notary in good standing with the Office of the Secretary of State is guilty of official misconduct and may be subject to a fine or imprisonment."

The Secretary of State shall cancel the appointment of all notaries whose commissions are returned to his office by the county clerks. No application fee will be refunded and no bonding company is required to issue a refund when an appointment is cancelled.

(As amended by Public Act 91-818, effective June 13, 2000)

ARTICLE III

Duties — Fees — Authority

* 3-101. Official Seal and Signature. (Effective June 1, 2009)

(a) Each notary public shall, upon receiving the commission from the county clerk, obtain an official rubber stamp seal with which the notary shall authenticate his official acts. The rubber stamp seal shall contain the following information:

(1) the words "Official Seal";

(2) the notary's official name;

(3) the words "Notary Public", "State of Illinois", and "My commission expires_____(commission expiration date)"; and

(4) a serrated or milled edge border in a rectangular form not more than

one inch in height by two and one-half inches in length surrounding the information.

(b) At the time of the notarial act, a notary public shall officially sign every notary certificate and affix the rubber stamp seal clearly and legibly using black ink, so that it is capable of photographic reproduction. The illegibility of any of the information required by this Section does not affect the validity of a transaction.

This subsection does not apply on or after July 1, 2013.

* 3-102. Notarial Record; Residential Real Property Transactions.
(Effective June 1, 2009)

(a) This Section shall apply to every notarial act in Illinois involving a document of conveyance that transfers or purports to transfer title to residential real property located in Cook County.

(b) As used in this Section, the following terms shall have the meanings ascribed to them:

(1) "Document of Conveyance" shall mean a written instrument that transfers or purports to transfer title effecting a change in ownership to Residential Real Property, excluding:

(i) court-ordered and court-authorized conveyances of Residential Real Property, including without limitation, quit-claim deeds executed pursuant to a marital settlement agreement incorporated into a judgment of dissolution of marriage, and transfers in the administration of a probate estate;

(ii) judicial sale deeds relating to Residential Real Property, including without limitation, sale deeds issued pursuant to proceedings to foreclose a mortgage or execute on a levy to enforce a judgment;

(iii) deeds transferring ownership of Residential Real Property to a trust where the beneficiary is also the grantor;

(iv) deeds from grantors to themselves that are intended to change the nature or type of tenancy by which they own Residential Real Property;

(v) deeds from a grantor to the grantor and another natural person that are intended to establish a tenancy by which the grantor and the other natural person own Residential Real Property;

(vi) deeds executed to the mortgagee in lieu of foreclosure of a mortgage; and

(vii) deeds transferring ownership to a revocable or irrevocable grantor trust where the beneficiary includes the grantor.

(2) "Financial Institution" shall mean a State or federally chartered bank, savings and loan association, savings bank, or credit union.

(3) "Notarial Record" shall mean the written document created in conformity with this Section by a notary in connection with Documents of Conveyance.

(4) "Residential Real Property" shall mean a building or buildings located in Cook County, Illinois and containing one to 4 dwelling units or an individual residential condominium unit.

(5) "Title Insurance Agent" shall have the meaning ascribed to it under the Title Insurance Act.

(6) "Title Insurance Company" shall have the meaning ascribed to it under the Title Insurance Act.

(c) A notary appointed and commissioned as a notary in Illinois shall, in addition to compliance with other provisions of this Act, create a Notarial Record of each notarial act performed in connection with a Document of Conveyance. The Notarial Record shall contain:

(1) The date of the notarial act;

(2) The type, title, or a description of the Document of Conveyance being notarized, and the property index number ("PIN") used to identify the Residential Real Property for assessment or taxation purposes and the common street address for the Residential Real Property that is the subject of the Document of Conveyance;

(3) The signature, printed name, and residence street address of each person whose signature is the subject of the notarial act and a certification by the person that the property is Residential Real Property as defined in this Section, which states "The undersigned grantor hereby certifies that the real property identified in this Notarial Record is Residential Real Property as defined in the Illinois Notary Public Act".

(4) A description of the satisfactory evidence reviewed by the notary to determine the identity of the person whose signature is the subject of the notarial act;

(5) The date of notarization, the fee charged for the notarial act, the Notary's home or business phone number, the Notary's residence street address, the Notary's commission expiration date, the correct legal name of the Notary's employer or principal, and the business street address of the Notary's employer or principal; and

(6) The notary public shall require the person signing the Document of Conveyance (including an agent acting on behalf of a principal under a duly executed power of attorney), whose signature is the subject of the notarial act, to place his or her right thumbprint on the Notarial Record. If the right thumbprint is not available, then the notary shall have the party use his or her left thumb, or any available finger, and shall so indicate on the Notarial Record. If the party signing the document is physically unable to provide a thumbprint or fingerprint, the notary shall so indicate on the Notarial Record and shall also provide an explanation of that physical condition. The notary may obtain the thumbprint by any means that reliably captures the image of the finger in a physical or electronic medium.

(d) If a notarial act under this Section is performed by a notary who is a principal, employee, or agent of a Title Insurance Company, Title Insurance Agent, Financial Institution, or attorney at law, the notary shall deliver the original Notarial Record to the notary's employer or principal within 14 days after the performance of the notarial act for retention for a period of 7 years as part of the employer's or principal's business records. In the event of a sale or merger of any of the foregoing entities or persons, the successor or assignee of the entity or person shall assume the responsibility to maintain the Notarial Record for the balance of the 7-year business records retention period. Liquidation or other cessation of activities in the ordinary course of business by any of the foregoing entities or persons shall relieve the entity or person from the obligation to maintain Notarial Records after delivery of Notarial Records to the Recorder of Deeds of Cook County, Illinois.

(e) If a notarial act is performed by a notary who is not a principal, employee, or agent of a Title Insurance Company, Title Insurance Agent, Financial Institution, or attorney at law, the notary shall deliver the original Notarial Record within 14 days after the performance of the notarial act to the Recorder of Deeds of Cook County, Illinois for retention for a period of 7 years, accompanied by a filing fee of $5.

(f) The Notarial Record required under subsection (c) of this Section shall be created and maintained for each person whose signature is the subject of a notarial act regarding a Document of Conveyance and shall be in substantially the following form:

NOTARIAL RECORD - RESIDENTIAL REAL PROPERTY TRANSACTIONS

Date Notarized:
Fee: $

The undersigned grantor hereby certifies that the real property identified in this Notarial Record is Residential Real Property as defined in the Illinois Notary Public Act.

Grantor's (Signer's) Printed Name:

Grantor's (Signer's) Signature:

Grantor's (Signer's) Residential Street Address, City, State, and Zip:

Type or Name of Document of Conveyance:

PIN No. of Residential Real Property:

Common Street Address of Residential Real Property:

Thumbprint or Fingerprint:

Description of Means of Identification:

Additional Comments:

Name of Notary Printed:

Notary Phone Number:

Commission Expiration Date:

Residential Street Address of Notary, City, State, and Zip:

Name of Notary's Employer or Principal:

Business Street Address of Notary's Employer or Principal, City, State, and Zip:

(g) No copies of the original Notarial Record may be made or retained by the Notary. The Notary's employer or principal may retain copies of the Notarial Records as part of its business records, subject to applicable privacy and confidentiality standards.

(h) The failure of a notary to comply with the procedure set forth in this Section shall not affect the validity of the Residential Real Property transaction in connection to which the Document of Conveyance is executed, in the absence of fraud.

(i) The Notarial Record or other medium containing the thumbprint or fingerprint required by subsection (c)(6) shall be made available or disclosed only upon receipt of a subpoena duly authorized by a court of competent jurisdiction. Such Notarial Record or other medium shall not be subject to disclosure under the Freedom of Information Act and shall not be made available to any other party, other than a party in succession of interest to the party maintaining the Notarial Record or other medium pursuant to subsection (d) or (e).

(j) In the event there is a breach in the security of a Notarial Record maintained pursuant to subsections (d) and (e) by the Recorder of Deeds of Cook County, Illinois, the Recorder shall notify the person identified as the "signer" in the Notarial Record at the signer's residential street address set forth in the Notarial Record. "Breach" shall mean unauthorized acquisition of the fingerprint data contained in the Notarial Record that compromises the security, confidentiality, or integrity of the fingerprint data maintained by the Recorder. The notification shall be in writing and made in the most expedient time possible and without unreasonable delay, consistent with any measures necessary to determine the scope of the breach and restore the reasonable security, confidentiality, and integrity of the Recorder's data system.

(k) Subsections (a) through (i) shall not apply on and after July 1, 2013.

(l) Beginning July 1, 2013, at the time of notarization, a notary public shall officially sign every notary certificate and affix the rubber stamp seal clearly and legibly using black ink, so that it is capable of photographic reproduction. The illegibility of any of the information required by this Section does not affect the validity of a transaction.

3-103. Notice.

(a) Every notary public who is not an attorney or an accredited immigration representative who advertises the services of a notary public in a language other than English, whether by radio, television, signs, pamphlets, newspapers, or other written communication, with the exception of a single desk plaque, shall post in the document, advertisement, stationery, letterhead, business card, or other comparable written material the following: notice in English and the language in which the advertisement appears. This notice shall be of a conspicuous size, if in writing, and shall state: "I AM NOT AN ATTORNEY LICENSED TO PRACTICE LAW IN ILLINOIS AND MAY NOT GIVE LEGAL ADVICE OR ACCEPT FEES FOR LEGAL ADVICE." If such advertisement is by radio or television, the statement may be modified but must include substantially the same message.

A notary public shall not, in any document, advertisement, stationery, letterhead, business card, or other comparable written material describing the role of the notary public, literally translate from English into another language terms or titles including, but not limited to, notary public, notary, licensed, attorney, lawyer, or any other term that implies the person is an attorney. To illustrate, the word "notario" is prohibited under this provision.

Failure to follow the procedures in this Section shall result in a fine of $1,000 for each written violation. The second violation shall result in suspension of notary authorization. The third violation shall result in permanent revocation of the commission of notary public. Violations shall not preempt or preclude additional appropriate civil or criminal penalties.

(b) All notaries public required to comply with the provisions of subsection (a) shall prominently post at their place of business as recorded with the Secretary of State pursuant to Section 2-102 of this Act a schedule of fees established by law which a notary public may charge. The fee schedule shall be written in English and in the non-English language in which notary services were solicited and shall contain the disavowal of legal representation required above in subsection (a), unless such notice of disavowal is already prominently posted.

(c) No notary public, agency or any other person who is not an attorney shall represent, hold themselves out or advertise that they are experts on immigration matters or provide any other assistance that requires legal analysis, legal judgment, or interpretation of the law unless they are a designated entity as defined pursuant to Section 245a.1 of Part 245a of the Code of Federal Regulations (8CFR 245a.1) or an entity accredited by the Board of Immigration Appeals.

(d) Any person who aids, abets or otherwise induces another person to give false information concerning immigration status shall be guilty of a Class A misdemeanor for a first offense and a Class 3 felony for a second or subsequent offense committed within 5 years of a previous conviction for the same offense.

Any notary public who violates the provisions of this Section shall be guilty of official misconduct and subject to fine or imprisonment.

Nothing in this Section shall preclude any consumer of notary public services from pursuing other civil remedies available under the law.

(e) No notary public who is not an attorney or an accredited representative shall accept payment in exchange for providing legal advice or any other assistance that requires legal analysis, legal judgment, or interpretation of the law.

(f) Violation of subsection (e) is a business offense punishable by a fine of 3 times the amount received for services, or $1,001 minimum, and restitution of the amount paid to the consumer. Nothing in this Section shall be construed to preempt nor preclude additional appropriate civil remedies or criminal charges available under law.

(g) If a notary public of this State is convicted of 2 or more business offenses involving a violation of this Act within a 12-month period while commissioned, or of 3 or more business offenses involving a violation of this Act within a 5-year period regardless of being commissioned, the Secretary shall automatically revoke the notary public commission of that person on the date that the person's most recent business offense conviction is entered as a final judgment. (As amended by Public Act 93-1001, effective August 23, 2004)

3-104. Maximum Fee. (*Effective June 1, 2009*)

(a) Except as provided in subsection (b) of this Section, the maximum fee in this State is $1.00 for any notarial act performed and, until July 1, 2013, up to $25 for any notarial act performed pursuant to Section 3-102.

*(b) Fees for a notary public, agency, or any other person who is not an attorney or an accredited representative filling out immigration forms shall be limited to the following:

*(1) $10 per form completion;

*(2) $10 per page for the translation of a non-English language into English where such translation is required for immigration forms;

*(3) $1 for notarizing;

*(4) $3 to execute any procedures necessary to obtain a document required to complete immigration forms; and

*(5) A maximum of $75 for one complete application.

Fees authorized under this subsection shall not include application fees required to be submitted with immigration applications.

Any person who violates the provisions of this subsection shall be guilty of a Class A misdemeanor for a first offense and a Class 3 felony for a second or subsequent offense committed within 5 years of a previous conviction for the same offense.

(c) Upon his own information or upon complaint of any person, the Attorney General or any State's Attorney, or their designee, may maintain an action for injunctive relief in the court against any notary public or any other person who violates the provisions of subsection (b) of this Section. These remedies are in addition to, and not in substitution for, other available remedies.

If the Attorney General or any State's Attorney fails to bring an action as provided pursuant to this subsection within 90 days of receipt of a complaint, any person may file a civil action to enforce the provisions of this subsection and maintain an action for injunctive relief.

(d) All notaries public must provide receipts and keep records for fees accepted for services provided. Failure to provide receipts and keep records that can be presented as evidence of no wrongdoing shall be construed as a presumptive admission of allegations raised in complaints against the notary for violations related to accepting prohibited fees.

---

*Only those notaries who are "designated entities" by the U.S. Citizenship and Immigration Service may perform these duties and charge these fees.

3-105. Authority.

A notary public shall have authority to perform notarial acts throughout the State so long as the notary resides in the same county in which the notary was commissioned or, if the notary is a resident of a state bordering Illinois, so long as the notary's principal place of work or principal place of business is in the same county in Illinois in which the notary was commissioned.

(As amended by Public Act 91-818, effective June 13, 2000)

3-106. Certificate of Authority.

Upon the receipt of a written request, the notarized document, and a fee of $2 payable to the Secretary of State or County Clerk, the Office of the Secretary of State or County Clerk shall provide a certificate of authority in substantially the following form:

I _____ (Secretary of State or _____ County Clerk) of the State of Illinois, which office is an office of record having a seal, certify that _____ (notary's name) by whom the foregoing or annexed document was notarized, was, on the _____ (insert date), appointed and commissioned a notary public in and for the State of Illinois and that, as such, full faith and credit is and ought to be given to this notary's official attestations. In testimony whereof, I have affixed my signature and the seal of this office this _____ (insert date).

_____ (Secretary of State or

_____ County Clerk).

ARTICLE IV

Change of Name or Move from County

4-101. Changes causing commission to cease to be in effect.

When any notary public legally changes his or her name or moves from the county in which he or she was commissioned or, if the notary public is a resident of a state bordering Illinois, no longer maintains a principal place of work or principal place of business in the same county in Illinois in which he or she was commissioned, the commission ceases to be in effect and should be returned to the Secretary of State. These individuals who desire to again become a notary public must file a new application, bond, and oath with the Secretary of State. (As amended by Public Act 91-818, effective June 13, 2000)

ARTICLE V

Reappointment as a Notary Public

5-101. Reappointment.

No person is automatically reappointed as a notary public. At least 60 days prior to the expiration of a commission the Secretary of State shall mail notice of the expiration date to the holder of a commission. Every notary public who is an applicant for reappointment shall comply with the provisions of Article II of this Act.

5-102. Solicitation to Purchase Bond.

No person shall solicit any notary public and offer to provide a surety bond more than 60 days in advance of the expiration date of the notary public's commission.

Nor shall any person solicit any applicant for a commission or reappointment thereof and offer to provide a surety bond for the notary commission unless any such solicitation specifically sets forth in bold face type not less than 1/4 inch in height the following: "WE ARE NOT ASSOCIATED WITH ANY STATE OR LOCAL GOVERNMENTAL AGENCY".

Whenever it shall appear to the Secretary of State that any person is engaged or is about to engage in any acts or practices which constitute or will constitute a violation of the provisions of this Section, the Secretary of State may, in his discretion, through the Attorney General, apply for an injunction, and, upon a proper showing, any circuit court shall have power to issue a permanent or temporary injunction or restraining order without bond to enforce the provisions of this Act, and either party to such suit shall have the right to prosecute an appeal from the order or judgment of the court.

Any person, association, corporation, or others who violate the provisions of this Section shall be guilty of a business offense and punishable by a fine of not less than $500 for each offense.

ARTICLE VI

Notarial Acts and Forms

6-101. Definitions.

(a) "Notarial act" means any act that a notary public of this State is authorized to perform and includes taking an acknowledgment, administering an oath or affirmation, taking a verification upon oath or affirmation, and witnessing or attesting a signature.

(b) "Acknowledgment" means a declaration by a person that the person has executed an instrument for the purposes stated therein and, if the instrument is executed in a representative capacity, that the person signed the instrument with proper authority and executed it as the act of the person or entity represented and identified therein.

(c) "Verification upon oath or affirmation" means a declaration that a statement is true and made by a person upon oath or affirmation.

(d) "In a representative capacity" means:

(1) for and on behalf of a corporation, partnership, trust, or other entity, as an authorized officer, agent, partner, trustee, or other representative;

(2) as a public officer, personal representative, guardian, or other representative, in the capacity recited in the instrument;

(3) as an attorney in fact for a principal; or

(4) in any other capacity as an authorized representative of another.

6-102. Notarial Acts. *(Effective June 1, 2009)*

(a) In taking an acknowledgment, the notary public must determine, either from personal knowledge or from satisfactory evidence, that the person appearing before the notary and making the acknowledgment is the person whose true signature is on the instrument.

(b) In taking a verification upon oath or affirmation, the notary public must determine, either from personal knowledge or from satisfactory evidence, that the person appearing before the notary and making the verification is the person whose true signature is on the statement verified.

(c) In witnessing or attesting a signature, the notary public must determine, either from personal knowledge or from satisfactory evidence, that the signature is that of the person appearing before the notary and named therein.

(d) A notary public has satisfactory evidence that a person is the person whose true signature is on a document if that person:

(1) is personally known to the notary;

(2) is identified upon the oath or affirmation of a credible witness personally known to the notary; or

(3) is identified on the basis of identification documents. Until July 1, 2013, identification documents are documents that are valid at the time of the notarial act, issued by a state or federal government agency, and bearing the photographic image of the individual's face and signature of the individual.

6-103. Certificate of Notarial Acts.

(a) A notarial act must be evidenced by a certificate signed and dated by the notary public. The certificate must include identification of the jurisdiction in which the notarial act is performed and the official seal of office.

(b) A certificate of a notarial act is sufficient if it meets the requirements of subsection (a) and it:

(1) is in the short form set forth in Section 6-105;

(2) is in a form otherwise prescribed by the law of this State; or

(3) sets forth the actions of the notary public and those are sufficient to meet the requirements of the designated notarial act.

6-104. Acts Prohibited.

(a) A notary public shall not use any name or initial in signing certificates other than that by which the notary was commissioned.

(b) A notary public shall not acknowledge any instrument in which the notary's name appears as a party to the transaction.

(c) A notary public shall not affix his signature to a blank form of affidavit or certificate of acknowledgment and deliver that form to another person with intent that it be used as an affidavit or acknowledgment.

(d) A notary public shall not take the acknowledgment of or administer an oath to any person whom the notary actually knows to have been adjudged mentally ill by a court of competent jurisdiction and who has not been restored to mental health as a matter of record.

(e) A notary public shall not take the acknowledgment of any person who is blind until the notary has read the instrument to such person.

(f) A notary public shall not take the acknowledgment of any person who does not speak or understand the English language, unless the nature and effect of the instrument to be notarized is translated into a language, which the person does understand.

(g) A notary public shall not change anything in a written instrument after it has been signed by anyone.

(h) No notary public shall be authorized to prepare any legal instrument, or fill in the blanks of an instrument, other than a notary certificate; however, this prohibition shall not prohibit an attorney, who is also a notary public, from performing notarial acts for any documents prepared by that attorney.

(i) If a notary public accepts or receives any money from any one to whom an oath has been administered or on behalf of whom an acknowledgment has been taken for the purpose of transmitting or forwarding such money to another and willfully fails to transmit or forward such money promptly, the notary is personally liable for any loss sustained because of such failure. The person or persons damaged by such failure may bring an action to recover damages, together with interest and reasonable attorney fees, against such notary public or his bondsmen.

(As amended by Public Act 85-421, effective January 1, 1988.)

6-105. Short Forms.

The following short form certificates of notarial acts are sufficient for the purposes indicated.

(a) For an acknowledgment in an individual capacity:

State of _____

County of _____

This instrument was acknowledged before me on _____ (date) by _____ (name/s of person/s.)

(seal) _____ (Signature of Notary Public)

(b) For an acknowledgment in a representative capacity:

State of _____

County of _____

This instrument was acknowledged before me on _____ (date) by _____ (name[s] of person[s]) as _____ (type of authority, e.g., officer, trustee, etc.) of _____ (name of party on behalf of whom instrument was executed).

(seal) _____ (Signature of Notary Public)

(c) For a verification upon oath or affirmation:

State of _____
County of _____

Signed and sworn (or affirmed) to before me on _____ (date) by _____ (name[s] of person[s] making statement).

(seal) _____ (Signature of Notary Public)

(d) For witnessing or attesting a signature:

State of _____
County of _____

Signed and attested before me on _____ (date) by _____ (name[s] of person[s]).

(seal) _____ (Signature of Notary Public)

ARTICLE VII

Liability and Revocation

7-101. Liability of Notary and Surety.
A notary public and the surety on the notary's bond are liable to the persons involved for all damages caused by the notary's official misconduct.

7-102. Liability of Employer of Notary.
The employer of a notary public is also liable to the persons involved for all damages caused by the notary's official misconduct, if:
(a) the notary public was acting within the scope of the notary's employment at the time the notary engaged in the official misconduct; and
(b) the employer consented to the notary's official misconduct.

7-103. Cause of Damages.

It is not essential to a recovery of damages that a notary's official misconduct be the only cause of the damages.

7-104. Official Misconduct Defined.

The term "official misconduct" generally means the wrongful exercise of a power or the wrongful performance of a duty and is fully defined in Section 33-3 of the Criminal Code of 1961. The term "wrongful" as used in the definition of official misconduct means unauthorized, unlawful, abusive, negligent, reckless, or injurious.

(As amended by Public Act 85-293, effective September 8, 1987)

7-105. Official Misconduct.

(a) A notary public who knowingly and willfully commits any official misconduct is guilty of a Class A misdemeanor.

(b) A notary public who recklessly or negligently commits any official misconduct is guilty of a Class B misdemeanor.

7-106. Willful Impersonation.

Any person who acts as, or otherwise willfully impersonates, a notary public while not lawfully appointed and commissioned to perform notarial acts is guilty of a Class A misdemeanor.

7-107. Wrongful Possession.

Any person who unlawfully possesses a notary's official seal is guilty of a misdemeanor and punishable upon conviction by a fine not exceeding $1,000.

7-108. Revocation of Commission.

The Secretary of State may revoke the commission of any notary public who, during the current term of appointment:

(a) submits an application for commission and appointment as a notary public which contains substantial and material misstatement or omission of fact; or

(b) is convicted of any felony, or official misconduct under this Act.

7-109. Action for Injunction, Unauthorized Practice of Law.

Upon his own information or upon complaint of any person, the Attorney General or any State's Attorney, or their designee, may maintain an action for injunctive relief in the circuit court against any notary public who renders, offers to render, or holds himself or herself out as rendering any service constituting the unauthorized practice of the law. Any organized bar association in this State may intervene in the action, at any stage of the proceeding, for good cause shown. The action may also be maintained by an organized bar association in this State. These remedies are in addition to, and not in substitution for, other available remedies.

UNIFORM RECOGNITION OF ACKNOWLEDGMENTS ACT

(As effective January 1, 1970)

(Illinois Revised Statutes Ch. 765 ILCS 30)

(765 ILCS 30/1) Sec. 1. Short title.

This Act may be cited as the Uniform Recognition of Acknowledgments Act. (Source: P. A. 76-1105.)

(765 ILCS 30/2) Sec. 2. Recognition of notarial acts performed outside this State.

For the purposes of this Act, "notarial acts" means acts which the laws and regulations of this State authorize notaries public of this State to perform, including the administering of oaths and affirmations, taking proof of execution and acknowledgments of instruments, and attesting documents. Notarial acts may be performed outside this State for use in this State with the same effect as if performed by a notary public of this State by the following persons authorized pursuant to the laws and regulations of other governments in addition to any other person authorized by the laws and regulations of this State:

(1) a notary public authorized to perform notarial acts in the place in which the act is performed;

(2) a judge, clerk, or deputy clerk of any court of record in the place in which the notarial act is performed;

(3) an officer of the foreign service of the United States, a consular agent, or any other person authorized by regulation of the United States Department of State to perform notarial acts in the place in which the act is performed;

(4) a commissioned officer in active service with the Armed Forces of the United States and any other person authorized by regulation of the Armed Forces to perform notarial acts if the notarial act is performed for one of the following or his dependents: a merchant seaman of the United States, a member of the Armed Forces of the United States, or any other person serving with or accompanying the Armed Forces of the United States; or

(5) any other person authorized to perform notarial acts in the place in which the act is performed. (Source: P. A. 76-1105.)

(765 ILCS 30/3) Sec. 3. Authentication of authority of officer.

(a) If the notarial act is performed by any of the persons described in paragraphs 1 to 4, inclusive of Section 2, other than a person authorized to perform notarial acts by the laws or regulations of a foreign country, the signature, rank, or title and serial number, if any, of the person are sufficient proof of the authority of a holder of that rank or title to perform the act. Further proof of his authority is not required.

(b) If the notarial act is performed by a person authorized by the laws or regulations of a foreign country to perform the act, there is sufficient proof of the authority of that person to act if:

(1) either a foreign service officer of the United States resident in the country in which the act is performed or a diplomatic or consular officer of the foreign country resident in the United States certifies that a person holding that office is authorized to perform the act;

(2) the official seal of the person performing the notarial act is affixed to the document; or

(3) the title and indication of authority to perform notarial acts of the person appears either in a digest of foreign law or in a list customarily used as a source of such information.

(c) If the notarial act is performed by a person other than one described in subsections (a) and (b), there is sufficient proof of the authority of that person to act if the clerk of a court of record in the place in which the notarial act is performed certifies to the official character of that person and to his authority to perform the notarial act.

(d) The signature and title of the person performing the act are prima facie evidence that he is a person with the designated title and that the signature is genuine. (Source: P.A. 76-1105.)

(765 ILCS 30/4) Sec. 4. Certificate of person taking acknowledgment.

The person taking an acknowledgment shall certify that:

(1) the person acknowledging appeared before him and acknowledged he executed the instrument; and

(2) the person acknowledging was known to the person taking the acknowledgment or that the person taking the acknowledgment had satisfactory evidence that the person acknowledging was the person described in and who executed the instrument. (Source: P.A. 91-357, eff. 7-29-99.)

(765 ILCS 30/5) Sec. 5. Recognition of certificate of acknowledgment.

The form of a certificate of acknowledgment used by a person whose authority is recognized under Section 2 shall be accepted in this State if:

(1) the certificate is in a form prescribed by the laws or regulations of this State;

(2) the certificate is in a form prescribed by the laws or regulations applicable in the place in which the acknowledgment is taken; or

(3) the certificate contains the words "acknowledged before me" or their substantial equivalent. (Source: P.A. 91-357, eff. 7-29-99.)

(765 ILCS 30/6) Sec. 6. Certificate of acknowledgment.

The words "acknowledged before me" means

(1) that the person acknowledging appeared before the person taking the acknowledgment,

(2) that he acknowledged he executed the instrument,

(3) that, in the case of:

(i) a natural person, he executed the instrument for the purposes therein stated;

(ii) a corporation, the officer or agent acknowledged he held the position or title set forth in the instrument and certificate, he signed the instrument on behalf of the corporation by proper authority, and the instrument was the act of the corporation for the purpose therein stated;

(iii) a partnership, the partner or agent acknowledged he signed the instrument on behalf of the partnership by proper authority and he executed the instrument as the act of the partnership for the purposes therein stated;

(iv) a person acknowledging as principal by an attorney in fact, he executed the instrument by proper authority as the act of the principal for the purposes therein stated;

(v) a person acknowledging as a public officer, trustee, administrator, guardian, or other representative, he signed the instrument by proper authority and he executed the instrument in the capacity and for the purposes therein stated; and

(4) that the person taking the acknowledgment either knew or had satisfactory evidence that the person acknowledging was the person named in the instrument or certificate. (Source: P. A. 76-1105.)

(765 ILCS 30/7) Sec. 7. Short forms of acknowledgment.

(a) The forms of acknowledgment set forth in this Section may be used and are sufficient for their respective purposes under any law of this State, whether executed in this State or any other State. The forms shall be known as "Statutory Short Forms of Acknowledgment" and may be referred to by that name. The authorization of the forms in this Section does not preclude the use of other forms.

(1) For an individual acting in his own right:

State of ....

County of ....

The foregoing instrument was acknowledged before me this (date) by (name of person acknowledged.)

(Signature of person taking acknowledgment)

(Title or rank)

(Serial number, if any)

(2) For a corporation:

State of ....

County of ....

The foregoing instrument was acknowledged before me this (date) by (name of officer or agent, title of officer or agent) of (name of corporation acknowledging) a (state or place of incorporation) corporation, on behalf of the corporation.

(Signature of person taking acknowledgment)

(Title or rank)

(Serial number, if any)

(3) For a partnership:
State of ....
County of ....

The foregoing instrument was acknowledged before me this (date) by (name of acknowledging partner or agent), partner (or agent) on behalf of (name of partnership), a partnership.

(Signature of person taking acknowledgment)

(Title or rank)

(Serial number, if any)

(4) For an individual acting as principal by an attorney in fact:

State of ....

County of ....

The foregoing instrument was acknowledged before me this (date) by (name of attorney in fact) as attorney in fact on behalf of (name of principal).

(Signature of person taking acknowledgment)

(Title or rank)

(Serial number, if any)

(5) By any public officer, trustee, or personal representative:
State of ....
County of ....

The foregoing instrument was acknowledged before me this (date) by (name and title of position).

(Signature of person taking acknowledgment)

(Title or rank)

(Serial number, if any)

(b) This amendatory Act of 1981 (P.A. 82-450) is to clarify that any uses of the short form of acknowledgment as herein provided within the State of Illinois prior to the effective date of this amendatory Act have been valid. (Source: P.A. 90-655, eff. 7-30-98.)

(765 ILCS 30/8) Sec. 8. Acknowledgments not affected by this Act.
A notarial act performed prior to the effective date of this Act is not affected by this Act. This Act provides an additional method of proving notarial acts. Nothing in this Act diminishes or invalidates the recognition accorded to notarial acts by other laws or regulations of this State. (Source: P. A. 76-1105.)

(765 ILCS 30/9) Sec. 9. Uniformity of interpretation.
This Act shall be so interpreted as to make uniform the laws of those states which enact it. (Source: P. A. 76-1105.)

(765 ILCS 30/10) Sec. 10. Time of taking effect.
This Act shall take effect on January 1, 1970. (Source: P.A. 76-1105.)

UNIFORM REAL PROPERTY ELECTRONIC RECORDING ACT

(765 ILCS 33/1) Sec. 1. Short title.
This Act may be cited as the Uniform Real Property Electronic Recording Act.
(Source: P.A. 95-472, eff. 8-27-07.)

(765 ILCS 33/2) Sec. 2. Definitions.
In this Act:
(1) "Document" means information that is:
(A) inscribed on a tangible medium or that is stored in an electronic or other medium and is retrievable in perceivable form; and (B) eligible to be recorded in the land records maintained by the county recorder.
(2) "Electronic" means relating to technology having electrical, digital, magnetic, wireless, optical, electromagnetic, or similar capabilities.
(3) "Electronic document" means a document that is received by the recorder in an electronic form.
(4) "Electronic signature" means an electronic sound, symbol, or process attached to or logically associated with a document and executed or adopted by a person with the intent to sign the document.

(5) "Person" means an individual, corporation, business trust, estate, trust, partnership, limited liability company, association, joint venture, public corporation, government, or governmental subdivision, agency, or instrumentality, or any other legal or commercial entity.

(6) "State" means a state of the United States, the District of Columbia, Puerto Rico, the United States Virgin Islands, or any territory or insular possession subject to the jurisdiction of the United States.

(7) "Secretary" means the Secretary of State.

(8) "Commission" means the Illinois Electronic Recording Commission. Any notifications required by this Act must be made in writing and may be communicated by certified mail, return receipt requested or electronic mail so long as receipt is verified.

(Source: P.A. 95-472, eff. 8-27-07.)

(765 ILCS 33/3) Sec. 3. Validity of electronic documents.

(a) If a law requires, as a condition for recording, that a document be an original, be on paper or another tangible medium, or be in writing, the requirement is satisfied by an electronic document satisfying this Act.

(b) If a law requires, as a condition for recording, that a document be signed, the requirement is satisfied by an electronic signature.

(c) A requirement that a document or a signature associated with a document be notarized, acknowledged, verified, witnessed, or made under oath is satisfied if the electronic signature of the person authorized to perform that act, and all other information required to be included, is attached to or logically associated with the document or signature. A physical or electronic image of a stamp, impression, or seal need not accompany an electronic signature.

(Source: P.A. 95-472, eff. 8-27-07.)

(765 ILCS 33/4) Sec. 4. Recording of documents.

(a) In this Section, "paper document" means a document that is received by the county recorder in a form that is not electronic.

(b) A county recorder:

(1) who implements any of the functions listed in this Section shall do so in compliance with standards established by the Illinois Electronic Recording Commission and must follow the procedures of the Local Records Act before destroying any original paper records as part of a conversion process into an electronic or other format.

(2) may receive, index, store, archive, and transmit electronic documents.

(3) may provide for access to, and for search and retrieval of, documents and information by electronic means, including the Internet, and on approval by the county recorder of the form and amount, the county board may adopt a fee for document detail or image retrieval on the Internet.

(4) who accepts electronic documents for recording shall continue to accept paper documents as authorized by State law and shall place entries for both types of documents in the same index.

(5) may convert paper documents accepted for recording into electronic form.

(6) may convert into electronic form information recorded before the county recorder began to record electronic documents.

(7) may accept electronically any fee or tax that the county recorder is authorized to collect.

(8) may agree with other officials of a state or a political subdivision thereof, or of the United States, on procedures or processes to facilitate the electronic satisfaction of prior approvals and conditions precedent to recording and the electronic payment of fees and taxes.

(Source: P.A. 95-472, eff. 8-27-07.)

(765 ILCS 33/5) Sec. 5. Administration and standards.

(a) To adopt standards to implement this Act, there is established, within the Office of the Secretary of State, the Illinois Electronic Recording Commission consisting of 15 commissioners as follows:

(1) The Secretary of State or the Secretary's designee shall be a permanent commissioner.

(2) The Secretary of State shall appoint the following additional 14 commissioners:

(A) Three who are from the land title profession.

(B) Three who are from lending institutions.

(C) One who is an attorney.

(D) Seven who are county recorders, no more than 4 of whom are from one political party, representative of counties of varying size, geography, population, and resources.

(3) On the effective date of this Act, the Secretary of State or the Secretary's designee shall become the Acting Chairperson of the Commission. The Secretary shall appoint the initial commissioners within 60 days and hold the first meeting of the Commission within 120 days, notifying commissioners of the time and place of the first meeting with at least 14 days' notice. At its first meeting the Commission shall adopt, by a majority vote, such rules and structure that it deems necessary to govern its operations, including the title, responsibilities, and election of officers. Once adopted, the rules and structure may be altered or amended by the Commission by majority vote. Upon the election of officers and adoption of rules or bylaws, the duties of the Acting Chairperson shall cease.

(4) The Commission shall meet at least once every year within the State of Illinois. The time and place of meetings to be determined by the Chairperson and approved by a majority of the Commission.

(5) Eight commissioners shall constitute a quorum.

(6) Commissioners shall receive no compensation for their services but may be reimbursed for reasonable expenses at current rates in effect at the Office of the Secretary of State, directly related to their duties as commissioners and participation at Commission meetings or while on business or at meetings which have been authorized by the Commission.

(7) Appointed commissioners shall serve terms of 3 years, which shall expire on December 1st. Five of the initially appointed commissioners, including at least 2 county recorders, shall serve terms of one year, 5 of the initially appointed commissioners, including at least 2 county recorders, shall

serve terms of 2 years, and 4 of the initially appointed commissioners shall serve terms of 3 years, to be determined by lot. The calculation of the terms in office of the initially appointed commissioners shall begin on the first December 1st after the commissioners have served at least 6 months in office.

(8) The Chairperson shall declare a commissioner's office vacant immediately after receipt of a written resignation, death, a recorder commissioner no longer holding the public office, or under other circumstances specified within the rules adopted by the Commission, which shall also by rule specify how and by what deadlines a replacement is to be appointed.

(c) The Commission shall adopt and transmit to the Secretary of State standards to implement this Act and shall be the exclusive entity to set standards for counties to engage in electronic recording in the State of Illinois.

(d) To keep the standards and practices of county recorders in this State in harmony with the standards and practices of recording offices in other jurisdictions that enact substantially this Act and to keep the technology used by county recorders in this State compatible with technology used by recording offices in other jurisdictions that enact substantially this Act, the Commission, so far as is consistent with the purposes, policies, and provisions of this Act, in adopting, amending, and repealing standards shall consider:

(1) standards and practices of other jurisdictions;

(2) the most recent standards promulgated by national standard-setting bodies, such as the Property Records Industry Association;

(3) the views of interested persons and governmental officials and entities;

(4) the needs of counties of varying size, population, and resources; and

(5) standards requiring adequate information security protection to ensure that electronic documents are accurate, authentic, adequately preserved, and resistant to tampering.

(e) The Commission shall review the statutes related to real property and the statutes related to recording real property documents and shall recommend to the General Assembly any changes in the statutes that the Commission deems necessary or advisable.

(f) Funding. The Secretary of State may accept for the Commission, for any of its purposes and functions, donations, gifts, grants, and appropriations of money, equipment, supplies, materials, and services from the federal government, the State or any of its departments or agencies, a county or municipality, or from any institution, person, firm, or corporation. The Commission may authorize a fee payable by counties engaged in electronic recording to fund its expenses. Any fee shall be proportional based on county population or number of documents recorded annually. On approval by a county recorder of the form and amount, a county board may authorize payment of any fee out of the special fund it has created to fund document storage and electronic retrieval, as authorized in Section 3-5018 of the Counties Code. Any funds received by the Office of the Secretary of State for the Commission shall be used entirely for expenses approved by and for the use of the Commission.

(g) The Secretary of State shall provide administrative support to the Commission, including the preparation of the agenda and minutes for Commission meetings, distribution of notices and proposed rules to commissioners, payment of bills and reimbursement for expenses of commissioners.

(h) Standards and rules adopted by the Commission shall be delivered to the Secretary of State. Within 60 days, the Secretary shall either promulgate by rule the standards adopted, amended, or repealed or return them to the Commission, with findings, for changes. The Commission may override the Secretary by a three-fifths vote, in which case the Secretary shall publish the Commission's standards.
(Source: P.A. 95-472, eff. 8-27-07.)

(765 ILCS 33/6) Sec. 6. (Blank).
(Source: P.A. 95-472, eff. 8-27-07.)

(765 ILCS 33/7) Sec. 7. Relation to Electronic Signatures in Global and National Commerce Act.
This Act modifies, limits, and supersedes the federal Electronic Signatures in Global and National Commerce Act (15 U.S.C. Section 7001, et seq.) but does not modify, limit, or supersede Section 101(c) of that Act (15 U.S.C. Section 7001(c)) or authorize electronic delivery of any of the notices described in Section 103(b) of that Act (15 U.S.C. Section 7003(b)).
(Source: P.A. 95-472, eff. 8-27-07.)

(765 ILCS 33/99) Sec. 99. Effective date.
This Act takes effect upon becoming law.
(Source: P.A. 95-472, eff. 8-27-07.)

Questions and Answers

1. **Q — I have mailed a notary application and bond to the Secretary of State. When may I begin notarizing documents?**
   A — An appointed notary public may begin notarizing documents when his or her commission has been recorded with the county clerk and he or she has obtained an official notary public seal.

2. **Q — May I notarize my own signature and/or the signatures of my spouse, children and other relatives?**
   A — A notary public may not notarize his or her own signature and may not notarize any document in which the notary's name appears as a party to the transaction. A notary may notarize the signature of his or her spouse, children and other relatives.

3. **Q — May I notarize documents that originate out of state?**
   A — Yes, as long as you perform the notarial act in Illinois and the notarial certificate indicates "State of Illinois, County of _____" to identify the jurisdiction in which the notarial act took place.

4. **Q — May I notarize documents when I am physically outside the State of Illinois?**
A — No. An Illinois notary public has the authority to perform notarial acts only while in the State of Illinois.

5. **Q — Should I charge a fee for my services as a notary public?**
A — The law does not require that you charge a fee. However, the maximum fee allowed is $1.*

6. **Q — Should I keep a log book of any actions as a notary?**
A — There is no requirement in Illinois that a notary public keep a log book or journal. However, a notary may keep one for his or her own record keeping.

7. **Q — How do I report a change in my home or work address or name while I am serving as a notary public?**
A — If you move or change employers and your new residence or place of employment is within the boundaries of the county from which you were appointed, you merely report the change of address to the Secretary of State. However, if you move out of the county or if you are a non-resident notary who changes employment to another county, you must resign your commission. Resignations should be submitted to the Secretary of State. You can then apply for a new appointment.

8. **Q — What are the most common errors or omissions made by notaries?**
A — (1) Failing to properly identify a person; (2) failing to administer an oath or affirmation (if required); and (3) failing to affix the notary seal.

9. **Q —If my notary appointment has expired and I have applied for a new appointment, may I continue to notarize documents?**
A — No. There is no grace period for a notary public once his or her appointment has expired. You may not perform notarial acts until you have recorded your new appointment with the county clerk and have obtained a new seal containing the date that your new term of office expires.

10. **Q — May I notarize documents that I will be signing as an officer on behalf of a corporation?**
A — No. You may never notarize your own signature, whether you are signing for yourself or for a corporation.

---

* Effective June 1, 2009 through June 30, 2013, Illinois Notaries may charge up to $25 for notarizations that require them to create a Notarial Record. (See "Notarial Record," pages 54-59.)

11. **Q — Can a notary give legal advice or prepare legal documents?**
A — No. A notary does not have this authority, unless he or she is also an attorney.

12. **Q — Can a notary give advice on immigration or fill out immigration forms?**
A — No. According to federal law, no person, unless an attorney, shall fill out legalization forms or applications related to the Immigration Reform and Control Act of 1986, unless he or she has been authorized to do so by the U.S. Citizenship and Immigration Service or the Board of Immigration Appeals.

13. **Q — Is notarization required by law?**
A — In many cases, yes. Some documents must be acknowledged before a notary, and other documents must be signed under oath to be effective. It is not a notary's duty to prepare the document, only to perform the notarial act and complete the notarial certificate.

14. **Q — How does a notary identify a signer?**
A — A Notary has satisfactory evidence if the person (1) is personally known to the notary; (2) is identified by a credible witness personally known to the notary; or (3) is identified on the basis of identification documents. Proper identification should include a photograph and a signature on a reliable identification card, such as a driver's license.*

15. **Q — How do I renew my notary appointment?**
A — There is no automatic reappointment in Illinois. You will be notified by the Secretary of State approximately 60 days prior to the date your appointment expires. A preprinted application and bond form will be enclosed with the notification if you wish to apply for appointment for another term.

16. **Q — My notary commission will soon expire, I have received a notice from a "Notary Association" with instructions on how to apply for reappointment. What is this association? I thought notary applications were approved by the Secretary of State.**
A — There are several groups operating in Illinois under the name of "notary association," "agency" or "company." They are private organizations and are not officially associated with any government agency. These organizations offer assistance to notaries, sell notary seals, and provide the $5,000 notary bond for a fee. Solicitations from these groups are required to contain the following

---

* Effective June 1, 2009 through June 30, 2013, Illinois Notaries may only accept identification documents that are current, issued by a state or federal government and contain a photograph and signature of the bearer. (See "Identification Documents," pages 38-40.)

statement: "WE ARE NOT ASSOCIATED WITH ANY STATE OR LOCAL GOVERNMENTAL AGENCY." Only you can decide where to purchase your surety bond. You can purchase a bond from most insurance companies, or you may want to purchase a bond from one of the notary associations or agencies. The Office of the Secretary of State does not make any recommendations.

17. **Q — May I notarize only in my own county?**
A — An Illinois notary public has the authority to act throughout the state if residing in the county from which he or she was appointed. The county in which the notarial act takes place should be inserted in the notarial certificate.

18. **Q — Must the person sign the document in my presence?**
A — If the document requires an oath (for example, the certificate reads "signed and sworn/affirmed before me…"), then an oath or affirmation must be administered to the person, and the person must sign the document in your presence. If the document requires acknowledgment, it is sufficient for the person to appear before you and acknowledge execution of the document. Never notarize an unsigned document. You may not take an acknowledgment because someone else assures you that the signature is genuine. You may not take an acknowledgment even when you recognize the signer's signature unless that person appears before you.

19. **Q — What should I do when a person for whom I have performed a notarial act requests proof that I am a notary?**
A — Occasionally, a "Certificate of Authority" is requested to be attached to a document that has been notarized, particularly when that document is being sent out of state. This certificate is proof that the notary was a commissioned notary on the date that the document was notarized. A "Certificate of Authority" may be obtained from the county clerk of the county in which your appointment is recorded or from the Secretary of State's office. It is not your responsibility, however, to obtain the certificate for the person. That person should contact the county clerk or the Secretary of State for information.

20. **Q — Is a notary responsible for the truth or accuracy of a document?**
A — No. The main purpose of notarization is to compel truthfulness by the signer. Notaries have no authority and are not required to verify the truth or accuracy of any document.

21. **Q — I would like to return to my maiden name. What does this involve?**
A — A person who change his or her name must resign his or her commission and apply for a new appointment.

22. **Q — I am a notary working in Illinois; however, we just moved across the state line into another state. May I continue to notarize when I am working at my job, which is in the State of Illinois?**

    A — No. Because you have moved out of state, you must resign your in-state notary commission. You must then reapply for a non-resident notary appointment, if you are eligible.

23. **Q — Where do I submit my resignation as a notary?**

    A — Resignations should be submitted to the Secretary of State, Index Department, 111 East Monroe Street, Springfield, Illinois 62756.

24. **Q — What could happen to someone who acts as a notary without a commission?**

    A — Performing unauthorized notarizations is a misdemeanor. The person could be fined or imprisoned for up to six months.

25. **Q — May notaries use rubber stamp signatures?**

    A — No. Notaries may not use facsimile signature stamps in signing his or her official certificates. A signature must be written in ink as commissioned. In addition, a facsimile signature may not be notarized.

26. **Q — What should be done with the notary stamp if a commission terminates through revocation, resignation or death?**

    A — The notary, or the notary's heirs, should destroy or deface the seal so that it may not be misused.

27. **Q — When does a notary's commission officially expire?**

    A — A notary receives a four-year appointment. A notary's commission expires at midnight of the expiration date of the appointment.

28. **Q — May a blank document be notarized?**

    A — Never notarize a blank or incomplete document. If a signer indicates that certain spaces in a document are to be left blank because they don't apply, suggest that he or she line through the spaces or write "Not Applicable" in them. This protects the signer from later unauthorized insertions, and it may prevent the notary from having to appear as a witness in a lawsuit.

29. **Q — Should I accept a notary certificate from the county clerk that contains errors?**

    A — No, return the certificate to the county clerk detailing the error and request a corrected certificate.

30. **Q — What information is required when requesting that a commission be cancelled?**

    A — A written request should contain (1) the name under which the commission was issued; (2) the commission number; (3) reason for the cancellation and any supporting documents; (4) home address and telephone number; (5) signature of the notary requesting cancellation; and (6) the date the request was made.

31. **Q — When does a non-resident commission expire?**
A — A non-resident commission is valid for one year from the effective date of the appointment.

32. **Q — How do I obtain an application to be commissioned as a non-resident notary?**
A — You must contact the Index Department at 217-782-7017 to request a non-resident applicant packet.

33. **Q — How do I report a change in my employer's address?**
A — If the change is within the county in which you are commissioned you must send a change of address to the Index Department in writing. However, if the new address is in a different county, you must resign your commission and re-apply.

34. **Q — Can my employer keep my seal and certificate if I leave the company?**
A — No. The seal and certificate are considered the property of the notary public. Also, if you lose possession of your seal, it is recommended that you resign your commission.

35. **Q — What should I do if my notary seal is stolen?**
A — Report the theft to the police. If for any reason you lose possession of your seal, it is recommended that you resign your commission.

36. **Q — Can information about any notary appointment be given to other people?**
A — Yes. Notary Public applications and appointments are public records available to any interested person for examination or copying.

37. **Q — Can notarizations be performed for minors?**
A — Yes, but the minor must be able to provide proof of identification, and a parent or legal guardian should be present.

38. **Q — My felony conviction was 20 years ago; can I apply for a notary public appointment?**
A — No. Individuals that have been convicted of a felony are not eligible to be commissioned as an Illinois Notary Public under the provisions set forth in the Notary Public Act. ■

Offices of the Illinois Secretary of State

Springfield
Office of the Secretary of State
Index Department
111 East Monroe Street
Springfield, IL 62756
Telephone: (217) 782-7017

Chicago
Office of the Secretary of State
17 N. State Street, Suite 1137
Chicago, IL 60602
Telephone: (312) 814-9219

In addition, there are many useful resources available at the state's official Web site, including links to legislation and the Secretary of State's office. You can access the Web site at: www. sos.state.il.us/departments/index/notary/home.html

County Clerks' Offices

Before the Notary's appointment is in effect, he or she must register the commission at the county clerk's office in the county in which the Notary resides or is employed. This must be done before the Notary can perform official acts.

For certified copies of marriage certificates, contact the county clerk in the county where the marriage took place.

Adams County
507 Vermont St
Quincy 62301
(217) 277-2150

Alexander County
2000 Washington Ave
Cairo 62914
(618) 734-7000

Bond County
203 W. College St
Greenville 62246
(618) 664-0449

Boone County
601 N. Main St, Ste 202
Belvidere 61008
(815) 544-3103

Brown County
200 Court St, Room 4
Mount Sterling 62353-0142
(217) 773-3421

Bureau County
700 S. Main St
Princeton 61356
(815) 875-2014

Calhoun County
P.O. Box 187
Hardin 62047
(618) 576-2351

Carroll County
301 N. Main St, P.O. Box 152
Mount Carroll 61053-0152
(815) 244-0221

Cass County
100 E. Springfield St
Virginia 62691
(217) 452-2277, Ext 4

Champaign County
1776 E. Washington St
Urbana 61802
(217) 384-3720

Christian County
P.O. Box 647
Taylorville 62568
(217) 824-4969

Clark County
501 Archer Ave
Marshall 62441
(217) 826-8311

Clay County
P.O. Box 160
Louisville 62858
(618) 665-3626

Clinton County
850 Fairfax St
P.O. Box 308
Carlyle 62231
(618) 594-2464

Coles County
651 Jackson, Room 122
Charleston 61920
(217) 348-0501

Cook County
Notary Dept.
118 N. Clark St
Chicago 60602
(312) 603-5648

Crawford County
100 Douglas St, P.O. Box 616
Robinson 62454
(618) 544-2590 or
(618) 546-1212

Cumberland County
P.O. Box 146
Toledo 62468
(217) 849-2631

DeKalb County
110 E. Sycamore St
Sycamore 60178
(815) 895-7149

DeWitt County
201 W. Washington
Clinton 61727
(217) 935-2119

Douglas County
401 S. Center St, P.O. Box 467
Tuscola 61953
(217) 253-2411

DuPage County
421 North County Farm Rd
Wheaton 60187
(630) 407-5500

Edgar County
115 W. Court St, Room J
Paris 61944
(217) 466-7433

Edwards County
50 E. Main St
Albion 62806
(618) 445-2115

Effingham County
101 N. 4th St, Ste. 201
P.O. Box 628
Effingham 62401
(217) 342-6535

Fayette County
P.O. Box 401
Vandalia 62471
(618) 283-5000

Ford County
200 W. State St, Room 101
Paxton 60957
(217) 379-2721

Franklin County
P.O. Box 607
Benton 62812
(618) 438-3221

Fulton County
100 N. Main St
Lewistown 61542
(309) 547-3041

Gallatin County
484 N Lincoln Blvd. W.
P.O. Box 550
Shawneetown 62984
(618) 269-3025

Greene County
519 N. Main
Carrollton 62016
(217) 942-5443

Grundy County
111 E. Washington St
P.O. Box 675
Morris 60450
(815) 941-3222

Hamilton County
100 S. Jackson St.
McLeansboro 62859
(618) 643-2721

Hancock County
P.O. Box 39
Carthage 62321
(217) 357-3911

Hardin County
P.O. Box 187
Elizabethtown 62931
(618) 287-2251

Henderson County
P.O. Box 308
Oquawka 61469
(309) 867-2911

Henry County
307 W. Center St
Cambridge 61238
(309) 937-3575

Iroquois County
1001 E. Grant St
Watseka 60970
(815) 432-6960

Jackson County
1001 Walnut St
Murphysboro 62966
(618) 687-7360

Jasper County
204 W. Washington, Ste 2
Newton 62448
(618) 783-3124

Jefferson County
100 S. 10th St, Room 105
Mount Vernon 62864
(618) 244-8020

Jersey County
200 N. Lafayette
Jerseyville 62052
(618) 498-5571 Ext. 115

JoDaviess County
300 N. Bench St
Galena 61036
(815) 777-0161

Johnson County
P.O. Box 96
Vienna 62995
(618) 658-3611

Kane County
719 S. Batavia Ave, Bldg B
Geneva 60134
(630) 232-5999

Kankakee County
189 E. Court St
Kankakee 60901
(815) 937-2990

Kendall County
111 W Fox St
Yorkville 60560
(630) 553-4104

Knox County
200 S. Cherry St
Galesburg 61401
(309) 345-3815

Lake County
18 N. County St, Room 1001
Waukegan 60085
(847) 377-2279

LaSalle County
707 E. Etna Rd
Ottawa 61350
(815) 434-8202

Lawrence County
1100 State St
Lawrence 62439
(618) 943-2346

Lee County
P.O. Box 329
Dixon 61021
(815) 288-3309

Livingston County
112 W. Madison St
Pontiac 61764
(815) 844-2006

Logan County
601 Broadway
P.O. Box 278
Lincoln 62656
(217) 732-4148

Macon County
141 S Main St, Room 104
Decatur 62523
(217) 424-1305

Macoupin County
P.O. Box 107
Carlinville 62626
(217) 854-3214

Madison County
157 N. Main St, Ste 109
Edwardsville 62025
(618) 692-6290

Marion County
P.O. Box 637
Salem 62881
(618) 548-3400

Marshall County
122 N. Prairie St
P.O. Box 328
Lacon 61540
(309) 246-6325

Mason County
P.O. Box 77
Havana 62644
(309) 543-6661

Massac County
1 Superman Sq, Room 2A
P.O. Box 429
Metropolis 62960
(618) 524-5213

McDonough County
1 Courthouse Sq
Macomb 61455
(309) 833-2474

McHenry County
2200 N. Seminary Ave
Woodstock 60098
(815) 334-4242

McLean County
115 E. Washington, #102
P.O. Box 2400
Bloomington 61701
(309) 888-5189 or
(309) 888-5190

Menard County
102 S. 7th St
P.O. Box 465
Petersburg 62675
(217) 632-3201

Mercer County
100 Southeast 3rd St
P.O. Box 66
Aledo 61231
(309) 582-7021

Monroe County
100 S. Main St
Waterloo 62298
(618) 939-8681 Ext. 302

Montgomery County
P.O. Box 595
Hillsboro 62049
(217) 532-9530

Morgan County
300 W. State St
P.O. Box 1387
Jacksonville 62650
(217) 243-8581

Moultrie County
10 S. Main St
Sullivan 61951
(217) 728-4389

Ogle County
P.O. Box 357
Oregon 61061
(815) 732-1110

Peoria County
324 Main St, Room 101
Peoria 61602
(309) 672-6059

Perry County
P.O. Box 438
Pinckneyville 62274
(618) 357-5116

Piatt County
101 W. Washington St
P.O. Box 558
Monticello 61856
(217) 762-9487

Pike County
100 E Washington St
Pittsfield 62363
(217) 285-6812

Pope County
P.O. Box 216
Golconda 62938
(618) 683-4466

Pulaski County
500 Illinois Ave
P.O. Box 118
Mound City 62963
(618) 748-9360

Putnam County
120 N. 4th St
P.O. Box 236
Hennepin 61327
(815) 925-7129

Randolph County
1 Taylor St, Room 202
Chester 62233
(618) 826-5000 Ext. 191

Richland County
103 W. Main St
Olney 62450
(618) 392-3111

Rock Island County
1504 3rd Ave
Rock Island 61201
(309) 558-3555

Saline County
10 E. Poplar St, Ste 17
Harrisburg 62946
(618) 253-8197

Sangamon County
200 S. 9th St, Room101
Springfield 62701
(217) 753-6740

Schuyler County
P.O. Box 200
Rushville 62681
(217) 322-4734

Scott County
23 E. Market St
Winchester 62694
(217) 742-3178

Shelby County
301 E. Main St
P.O. Box 230
Shelbyville 62565
(217) 774-4421

St. Clair County
10 Public Square
Belleville 62220
(618) 277-6600

Stark County
130 W. Main St
P.O. Box 97
Toulon 61483
(309) 286-5911

Stephenson County
15 N. Galena Ave, Ste. 2
Freeport 61032
(815) 235-8289

Tazewell County
11 S. 4th St, Room 203
Pekin 61554
(309) 477-2264

Union County
309 W. Market, Room 100
Jonesboro 62952
(618) 833-5711

Vermilion County
6 N. Vermilion St
Danville 61832
(217) 554-1900

Wabash County
P.O. Box 277
Mount Carmel 62863
(618) 262-4561

Warren County
100 W. Broadway
Monmouth 61462
(309) 734-4612

Washington County
101 E. St. Louis St
Nashville 62263
(618) 327-4800 Ext. 300

Wayne County
P.O. Box 187
Fairfield 62837
(618) 842-5182

White County
301 E. Main St
P.O. Box 339
Carmi 62821
(618) 382-7211, Ext. 1

Whiteside County
200 E. Knox St
Morrison 61270
(815) 772-5189

Will County
302 N. Chicago St
Joliet 60432
(815) 740-4615

Williamson County
200 W. Jefferson
P.O. Box 1108
Marion 62959
(618) 997-1301, Ext. 121

Winnebago County
404 Elm St, Room 104
Rockford 61101
(815) 987-3050

Woodford
115 N. Main St, Room 202
Eureka 61530
(309) 467-2822

Bureaus of Vital Statistics

Illinois Notaries are not permitted to make certified copies of any document, and particularly not of such vital records as birth, death, or marriage certificates, and divorce decrees. Persons requesting "notarization," "certification" or certified copies of such documents should be referred to the appropriate public bureau of vital statistics. The following state agencies can provide certified copies of birth and death records for persons who were born or have died in the respective states, as can certain local offices not listed here:

Alabama
Vital Records
Department of Public Health
P.O. Box 5625
Montgomery, AL 36103-5625

Alaska
Bureau of Vital Statistics
Dept. of Health & Social Services
5441 Commercial Bl.
Juneau, AK 99801

Arizona
Office of Vital Records
Dept. of Health Services
P.O. Box 3887
Phoenix, AZ 85030-3887

Arkansas
Division of Vital Records
Department of Health
4815 West Markham Street, Slot 44
Little Rock, AR 72205-3867

California
Office of Vital Records
Department of Health Services
P.O. Box 997410, MS: 5103
Sacramento, CA 95899-7410

Colorado
Health Statistics
Department of Health
CHEIS-HS-A1
4300 Cherry Creek Drive South
Denver, CO 80246-1530

Connecticut
CT Department of Public Health
State Office of Vital Records
410 Capitol Ave., MS#11VRS
P.O. Box 340308
Hartford, CT 06134-0308

Delaware
Delaware Health Statistics Center
Office of Vital Statistics
Jesse S. Cooper Building
417 Federal Street
Dover, DE 19901

District of Columbia
Department of Health
John A. Wilson Building
1350 Pennsylvania Avenue NW
Washington, DC 20004

Florida
Department of Health
Office of Vital Statistics
4052 Bald Cypress Way
Tallahassee, FL 32399-1701

Georgia
Vital Records
2600 Skyland Drive NE
Atlanta, GA 30319-3640

Hawaii
State Department of Health
Vital Statistics Section
P.O. Box 3378
Honolulu, HI 96801

Idaho
Department of Health and
    Welfare
Vital Statistics Unit
450 West State Street, 1st Floor
P.O. Box 83720
Boise, ID 83720

Illinois
Health Statistics
Department of Public Health
605 West Jefferson Street
Springfield, IL 62702-5097

Indiana
Vital Records Department
Indiana State Department of
    Health
6 West Washington Street
Indianapolis, IN 46204

Iowa
Department of Public Health
Bureau of Vital Records
Lucas Office Building, 1st Floor
321 East 12th Street
Des Moines, IA 50319-0075

Kansas
Office of Vital Statistics
1000 SW Jackson Street, Suite 120
Topeka, KS 66612

Kentucky
Office of Vital Statistics
Department for Health Services
275 East Main Street-IE-A
Frankfort, KY 40621-0001

Louisiana
Vital Records Registry
P.O. Box 60630
New Orleans, LA 70160

Maine
Department of Human Services
Vital Records
221 State Street, Station 11
11 State House Station
Augusta, ME 04333-0011

Maryland
Division of Vital Records
6550 Reisterstown Plaza
Reiserstown Road Plaza
Baltimore, MD 21215

Massachusetts
Vital Records and Statistics
150 Mt. Vernon Street, First Floor
Dorchester, MA 02125-3105

Michigan
Department of Community
    Health
3423 N. Martin Luther King Blvd.
P.O. Box 30721
Lansing, MI 48909

Minnesota
Minnesota Department of Health
Attention: Office of the State
    Registrar
P.O. Box 64882
St. Paul, MN 55164-0882

Mississippi
Vital Records
571 Stadium Drive
P.O. Box 1700
Jackson, MS 39215-1700

Missouri
Department of Health
Bureau of Vital Records
930 Wildwood
P.O. Box 570
Jefferson City, MO 65102

Montana
Office of Vital Statistics
Department of Public Health
P.O. Box 4210
111 North Sanders, Room 209
Helena, MT 59604

Nebraska
Vital Statistics
Department of Health
P.O. Box 95044
Lincoln, NE 68509-5044

Nevada
Office of Vital Records
4150 Technology Way, Suite 104
Carson City, Nevada 89706

New Hampshire
NH Department of State
Division of Vital Records
    Administration
71 South Fruit Street
Concord, NH 03301-2410

New Jersey
Vital Statistics
Customer Service Unit
P.O. Box 370
Trenton, NJ 08625-0370

New Mexico
Vital Records and Health
    Statistics
P.O. Box 26110
1105 St. Francis Drive
Santa Fe, NM 87502

New York
Certification Unit
Vital Records Section
800 North Pearl Street, 2nd Floor
Menands, NY 12204

New York City
New York State Department of
    Health
Vital Records Section
Certification Unit
P.O. Box 2602
Albany, NY 12220-2602

North Carolina
Vital Records
1903 Mail Service Center
Raleigh, NC 27699-1903

North Dakota
Division of Vital Records
600 East Boulevard Ave.
Department 301
Bismarck, ND 58505-0200

Ohio
Ohio Department of Health
Vital Statistics
P.O. Box 15098
Columbus, OH 43215-0098

Oklahoma
Vital Records Service
State Department of Health
1000 Northeast Tenth, Room 111
Oklahoma City, OK 73117

Oregon
Oregon Vital Records
800 NE Oregon Street, Ste 205
P.O. Box 14050
Portland, OR 97293

Pennsylvania
Vital Records
State Department of Health
101 S. Mercer Street
P.O. Box 1528
New Castle, PA 16101

Rhode Island
Office of Vital Records
Department of Health
3 Capitol Hill
Room 101
Providence, RI 02908-5097

South Carolina
Office of Vital Records
2600 Bull Street
Columbia, SC 29201

South Dakota
Vital Records
207 E. Missouri Ave., Suite #1A
Pierre, SD 57501

Tennessee
Vital Records
Central Services Building
1st Floor
421 5th Avenue North
Nashville, TN 37247

Texas
Bureau of Vital Statistics
Department of Health
P.O. Box 12040
Austin, TX 78711-2040

Utah
Vital Records & Statistics
Cannon Health Building
288 North 1460 West
P.O. Box 141012
Salt Lake City, UT 84114-1012

Vermont
Department of Health
Vital Records Section
108 Cherry Street
P.O. Box 70
Burlington, VT 05402-0070

Virginia
Office of Vital Records
P.O. Box 1000
Richmond, VA 23218

Washington
Department of Health
Center for Health Statistics
P.O. Box 9709
Olympia, WA 98507-9709

West Virginia
Vital Registration Office
350 Capitol Street, Room 165
Charleston, WV 25301-3701

Wisconsin
Vital Records
1 West Wilson Street
P.O. Box 309
Madison, WI 53701-0309

Wyoming
Vital Records Services
Hathaway Building
Cheyenne, WY 82002

American Samoa
American Samoa Office of
    Records and Vital Statistics
LBJ Tropical Medical Center
Department of Health Services
American Samoa Government
Pago Pago, AS 96799

Guam
Department of Public Health
    and Social Services
Government of Guam
P.O. Box 2816
Agana, GU M.I. 96932

Northern Mariana Islands
Bureau of Health Planning
Vital Statistics Office
P.O. Box 500409 CK
Saipan, MP 96950-0409

Panama Canal Zone
Vital Records Section
Passport Services
U.S. Department of State
1111 19th Street NW, Suite 510
Washington, DC, CZ 34011-2300

Puerto Rico
Department of Health
Demographic Registry
P.O. Box 11854
Fernández Juncos Station
San Juan, PR 00910

Virgin Islands (St. Croix)
Department of Health
Vital Statistics
Charles Harwood Memorial
    Complex
Christiansted, St. Croix, VI 00820

**Virgin Islands (St. Thomas,
St. John)**
Department of Health
Vital Statistics
Old Municipal Hospital
St. Thomas, VI 00802

Hague Convention Nations

The nations listed on the following pages are parties to a treaty called the *Hague Convention Abolishing the Requirement of Legalization (Authentication) for Foreign Public Documents.*

Treaty Simplifies Authentication. A Notary's signature on documents that are sent to these nations may be authenticated (verified as valid for the benefit of the recipient in the foreign nation) through attachment of a single certificate of capacity called an apostille. The *apostille* (French for "notation") is the only authentication certificate necessary. Nations not subscribing to the Hague Convention may require as many as five or six separate authenticating certificates from different governmental agencies, domestic and foreign.

How to Request an *Apostille*. To obtain an *apostille*, mail the notarized document, a self-addressed stamped envelope and a $2 check payable to the "Secretary of State" to:

> Department of Index
> 111 East Monroe Street
> Springfield, IL 62756

An *apostille* must be specifically requested, indicating the nation to which the document will be sent. It is not the Notary's responsibility to obtain an *apostille*, but rather, it is the responsibility of the party needing authentication.

Hague Convention Nations. The following nations participate in the Hague Convention:

Albania	Fiji[10]
Andorra[10]	Finland
Antigua and Barbuda[10]	France[3]
Argentina[1]	Georgia
Armenia[10]	Germany
Australia	Greece
Austria	Grenada[10]
Azerbaijan	Honduras[10]
Bahamas[10]	Hong Kong[4]
Barbados[10]	Hungary
Belarus	Iceland
Belgium	India
Belize[10]	Ireland
Bosnia-Herzegovina[2]	Israel
Botswana[10]	Italy
Brunei Darussalam[10]	Japan
Bulgaria	Kazakhstan[10]
Colombia[10]	Latvia
Cook Islands	Lesotho[10]
Croatia[2]	Liberia[5 and 10]
Cyprus	Liechtenstein[10]
Czech Republic	Lithuania
Denmark	Luxembourg
Dominica[10]	Macao[4]
Ecuador	Macedonia[2]
El Salvador[10]	Malawi[10]
Estonia	Malta

---

1. Excludes recognition of extension of the Convention by the United Kingdom to the Malvinas (Falkland Islands), South Georgia, South Sandwich Islands and the Argentine Antarctic Sector.

2. The former Yugoslavia was a party to the Convention. Only the breakaway nations of Bosnia-Herzegovina, Croatia, Macedonia, Montenegro, Serbia and Slovenia have confirmed that the Convention still applies.

3. Including *Comoros Islands, Djibouti*, French Guyana, French Polynesia, Guadeloupe, Martinique, New Caledonia, Reunion, St. Pierre and Miquelon and Wallis and Futuna. (Names appearing in regular type denote territories; *italic type denotes now-independent nations that have not affirmed participation in the Convention.*)

4. Retained status as Hague nation after control was returned to China on July 1, 1997 (Hong Kong) and December 20, 1999 (Macao).

5. The Convention does not apply between Liberia and the United States.

Marshall Islands[10]
Mauritius[10]
Mexico
Moldova
Monaco
Montenegro[2]
Namibia[10]
Netherlands[6]
New Zealand
Niue[10]
North Korea
Norway
Panama
Poland
Portugal[7]
Romania
Russian Federation
Saint Kitts and Nevis[10]
Saint Lucia[10]
Saint Vincent and
   the Grenadines[10]

Samoa[10]
San Marino[10]
São Tomé e Principe
Serbia[2]
Seychelles[10]
Slovakia
Slovenia[2]
South Africa
Spain
Suriname
Swaziland[10]
Sweden
Switzerland
Tonga[10]
Trinidad and Tobago[10]
Turkey
Ukraine
United Kingdom[8]
United States[5 and 9]
Vanuatu
Venezuela

Inquiries. Persons with questions about the *Hague Convention Abolishing the Requirement of Legalization for Foreign Public Documents* may address their inquiries to:

> Authentication Office
> 518 23rd Street, N.W.
> State Annex 1
> Washington, DC 20037
> (202) 647-5002

---

6. Extended to all Aruba, Curacao and Netherlands Antilles.

7. Extended to Angola, Mozambique and all overseas territories.

8. United Kingdom of Great Britain and Northern Ireland is extended to Anguilla, Bermuda, British Antarctica Territory, British Virgin Islands, Cayman Islands, Falkland Islands, Gibraltar, Guyana, Guernsey, Isle of Man Jersey, Kiribati, Montserrat, St. Helena, Solomon Islands, Turks and Caicos Islands, *Tuvalu, Vanuatu and Zimbabwe. (Names appearing in regular type denote territories; italic type denotes now-independent nations that have not affirmed participation in the Convention.)*

9. Includes American Samoa, District of Columbia, Guam, Northern Mariana Islands, Puerto Rico and U.S. Virgin Islands.

10. This country is not a member of the *Hague Conference on Private International Law* but has signed the *Hague Convention Abolishing the Requirement of Legalization for Foreign Public Documents.*

About the NNA

Since 1957, the National Notary Association — a nonprofit educational organization — has served the nation's Notaries Public with a wide variety of instructional programs and services.

As the country's clearinghouse for information on notarial laws, customs and practices, the NNA educates Notaries through publications, seminars, annual conferences and a Notary Information Service that offers immediate answers to specific questions about notarization.

The Association is perhaps most widely known as the preeminent source of information for and about Notaries. NNA works include:

• *The National Notary*, a magazine for National Notary Association members featuring how-to articles and practical tips on notarizing.

• *Notary Bulletin* newspaper, keeping NNA members up to date on developments affecting Notaries, especially new state laws and regulations.

• *Notary Basics Made Easy*, a first-of-its-kind video instruction program that simplifies Notary practices and procedures.

• *Notary Home Study Course*, a work-at-your-own-speed course covering every facet of notarization.

• *Sorry, No Can Do!* series, four volumes that help Notaries explain to customers and bosses why some requests for notarizations are improper and cannot be accommodated.

- *U.S. Notary Reference Manual*, invaluable for any person relying upon the authenticity and correctness of legal documents.

- *Notary Public Practices & Glossary*, widely hailed as the Notary's bible, a definitive reference book on notarial procedures.

- *State Notary Law Primers*, explaining a state's notarial statutes in easy-to-understand language.

- *The Model Notary Act*, prototype legislation conceived in 1973 and updated in 1984 and 2002 by an NNA-recruited panel of secretaries of state, legislators and attorneys, and regularly used by state legislatures in revising their notarial laws.

- *Notary Law & Practice: Cases & Materials*, the definitive and one-of-a-kind text for teaching Notary law to law students in schools and to attorneys in Minimum Continuing Education Seminars (MCLE), discussing every major judicial decision affecting the Notary's duties.

- *Notary Signing Agent Certification Course*, invaluable for candidates preparing to complete the Notary Signing Agent Certification Examination developed by the National Notary Association.

- Public-service pamphlets informing the general public about the function of a Notary, including *What Is A Notary Public?*, printed in English and Spanish.

In addition, the National Notary Association offers the highest quality professional supplies, including official seals and stamps, embossers, recordkeeping journals, affidavit stamps, thumbprinting devices and notarial certificates.

Though dedicated primarily to educating and assisting Notaries, the National Notary Association devotes part of its resources to helping lawmakers draft effective notarial statutes and to informing the public about the Notary's vital role in modern society. ■

Index

A

Acknowledgment. 24, **26–28**
78, *94*
   Acknowledge signature . . **26–28**
   Attorney in fact, by . . **27**, *94–95*
   Certificates **27–28**, *78–79*
96–97
   Credible identifying
     witness, for **39–40**, *95*
   Fees **47**, *92*
   Identification of signer. . . .27, 28
37–40, *95*
   Individual, by **28**, *96*
   Purpose. 27
   Representative, by . . . **27**, *96–97*
   Representative capacity **27**
96–97
   Requirements 26–28
   Terminology 28
   Witnessing signature 12–13
28, *110*
Address, change of **23**, *77–78*
93, 108, 112
Advertising **26**, 52, 65
82, 90–92
   Foreign language. . . . 26, **52**, 65
82, 90–92
   Immigration. **26**, 65, *90–92*
Advice **49–50**, 53, 53–54
Affidavit **33–34**
   Certificate for. **31**, *97*

Document custodian, for . . 32–33
   Fees **47**, *92*
   Immigration, for 53
   Oath or affirmation for. 34
   Purpose. 30–31
Affirmation 24, **29–30**, 40
79–80, 94–95
   Affidavit, for **29**, 31
   Ceremony 30
   Credible identifying
     witness, for 40, *95*
   Defined. 29–30
   Fees **47**, 77, *92*
   Gestures 30
   Power to administer. 29
   Purpose. 29
   Response required. 30
   Subscribing witness, for 36
   Verification, for **32**, *79–80*
97
   Wording 29–30
Apostilles **62–63**, 125–127
   Out of country. 62–63
   Procedure **62–63**, 125–127
Appointment, Notary . . 3–5, **19–24**
75–76, 84, 107–112
   Address, change of 21, 23
77–78, 93, 108, 112
   Application for 3–4, **19–20**
66, 75–76, 84

Bond. 4, **20–21**, 66–67, *85*
Cancellation of **22**, *77*
           111–112
Certificate of 4–5, **21–22**
Death of Notary. 24
Fees 4, **19–20**, *84–85*
Jurisdiction 22, *77, 93*
Liability. **21**, *97–98*
Name, change of **23**, *77–78*
           93, 108
Nonresidents. **19–20**, *75*
         75–76, 112
Oath for 21, *85*
Qualifications 3, **19–20**
         75, 84
Renewal 3, *78, 93–94, 109*
Resident-alien Notaries. 3
         19–20
Resignation **23**, 47, *111*
Revocation 3–4, 47, **66**
         78, 98
Term. 3–4, **22–23**, *78*
Authentication. . . . **62–63**, 125–127
Apostilles 62–63
Hague Convention. 62–63
         125–127
Out of country. 62–63
Out of state 62
Procedure 62–63
Authenticity, certificate of
(*See* Authentication)
Authority, certificate of. 62–63

B
Beneficial interest 49
Birth certificates, notarizing **12**
         32
Blank spaces in document . . **25**, *64*
Bond, Notary. 4, **20–21**
         66–67, *76, 97*
Change of name or county 21
Filing 4–5, **20**, *76*

Protects public. **20–21**
         66–67
Requirement 20, *76*
Surety **20–21**, *76*
Bureaus of Vital
Statistics. 120–124

C
Capacity, certificate of
(*See* Authentication)
Capacity of signer **27**, *96–97*
Certificate of appointment 5
         21–22, *75–76*
Certificate of
authentication 62–63
Certificate of authority 62–63
Certificate of capacity. 62–63
Certificate of prothonotary . . 62–63
Certificates, notarial 8, 16–17
         43–45, *78–80, 96–97*
Acknowledgment. . . . **27–28**, *79*
         96–97
Blank **64**, *95*
Choosing. **17–18**, 45
Contents 43–44
Copy certification by
document custodian. . . 32–33
Loose certificates 17, **44–45**
Military-officer 60
Pre-sign/pre-seal 45
Proof of execution by
subscribing witness . . . 36–37
Requirement **43–44**, *78, 95*
Seal of Notary 44
Signature by mark . . . **50–51**, *81*
Signature of Notary 44, *77*
Statement of particulars . . 43–44
Testimonium clause 44
Venue 43
Verification upon oath
or affirmation. **31**, *79–80*
         97

Page numbers listed in **bold** indicate where the most complete information on a subject can be found. *Italics* indicate pages where the statutes and state-published information pertaining to a subject are located.

Witnessing signature 35
Commission
(*See* Appointment, Notary)
Competence, determining . . **14–15**
25, 53
Conformed copy 11
Copy certification by
document custodian 32–33
Certificate 32–33

Procedure 32
Purpose. 32
Vital records, not for 32
County clerk's offices. . . . 114–119
Credible identifying witness 10
37, **39–40**
95

Affirmation for. 40
Identification of 39–40
Oath for 40
Purpose. 39
Qualifications 39–40
Signature in journal 40
Customers, restricting
services to 11–12

D
Date of document 16
Death certificates, notarizing . . . 12
32
Disqualifying interest 13, **49**
95, *107*
Beneficial interest 13, **49**
Financial interest 13, **49**
Impartiality 13, **49**
Influence. 13
Relatives 13, **49**, *107*
Documents
Dates, checking. 16
Foreign language. 12, **52**
Immigration. 53
Incomplete **15**, *111*
Preparation of 26, **49–50**
96
Scan for information 15–16

Selection of 49–50
Duties of Notary **24–25**
74–81

E
Electronic signatures 63–64
Embosser 6–7
Equipment 6–8
Errors and omissions
insurance. 8
Exam, practice. 68–73

F
Family members,
notarizing for 13, **49**, *107*
Faxes, notarizing 11
Fees **47–48**, 77, *92*
Acknowledgments **47**, 77
Affirmations. **47**, 77
Appointment. 3–5, **19–22**
75–76, *84*
Employee Notaries. 11
Immigration papers **47–48**
92
Maximum 47–48
Notarial record **48**, *92*
Oaths **47**, 77, *92*
Option not to charge 48
Overcharging. 48
Posting **48**, *90–92*
Proof of execution by
subscribing witness . . . **47**, 77
Schedule. 48, *90–92*
Travel 48
Verifications. 47, 77
Felony (*See* Misconduct)
Financial interest 13, **49**
Fines (*See* Misconduct)
Flags (*See* Authentication)
Foreign languages 12, 26
52–53, 65
Advertising 26, **52**, 65, *82*
90–92
Documents 12, **52**
Signers 53

H

Hague Convention. 62–63
125–127
Nations 126–127

I

Identification. 10, 14, **37–40**
51, *78, 95, 109*
Acceptable identification
documents. 14, **38–39**
95
Acknowledgment. . . . **37–40**, *78*
95, 109
Credible identifying
witness 10, 37, **39–40**
78, 95, 109
Minors. 51
Personal knowledge **37–38**
78, 95, 109
Procedure 37–40
Satisfactory evidence **37**, *78*
95, 109
Subscribing witness **36**
37–40, *78*
95, 109
Verification upon oath
or affirmation. **37–40**, *78*
95, 109
Witnessing a signature . . . **37–40**
78, 95, 109
Illinois Compiled Statutes. . *83–102*
5 ILCS 1-101 . . . .*83*
5 ILCS 1-102 . . . .*83*
5 ILCS 1-103 . . . .*83*
5 ILCS 1-104 . . . . *83–84*
5 ILCS 2-101 . . . . **20**, 22, *84*
5 ILCS 2-102 . . . . **19–20**, 66, *84*
5 ILCS 2-103 . . . . **20**, *84*
5 ILCS 2-104 . . . . **21**, *85*
5 ILCS 2-105 . . . . 20, *85*
5 ILCS 2-106 . . . . **21–22**, *85–86*
5 ILCS 3-101 . . . . **45–46**, *86–87*

5 ILCS 3-102 . . . . .**54–59**, 65–66
87–90
5 ILCS 3-103 . . . . .26, 48, **49–50**
52, *90–92*
5 ILCS 3-104 . . . . . . **47–48**, *92*
5 ILCS 3-105 . . . .*93*
5 ILCS 3-106 . . . . **62–63**, *93*
5 ILCS 4-101 . . . . 21, **23**, *93*
5 ILCS 5-101 . . . . *93–94*
5 ILCS 5-102 . . . .*94*
5 ILCS 6-101 . . . . .**24–25**, 27, 29
94–95
5 ILCS 6-102 . . . . 31, **37–40**, *95*
5 ILCS 6-103 . . . .*95*
5 ILCS 6-104 . . . . *95–96*
5 ILCS 6-105 . . . . .27–28, 31
35, *96–97*
5 ILCS 7-101 . . . . .21, 66–67, *97*
5 ILCS 7-102 . . . . 66, *97*
5 ILCS 7-103 . . . .*98*
5 ILCS 7-104 . . . .*98*
5 ILCS 7-105 . . . . **67**, *98*
5 ILCS 7-106 . . . . . . **24**, 67, *98*
5 ILCS 7-107 . . . . . . **47**, 67, *98*
5 ILCS 7-108 . . . . **66**, *98*
5 ILCS 7-109 . . . .*98*
765 ILCS 30/1 . . . .*99*
765 ILCS 30/2 . . . .24–25, **35**, *99*
765 ILCS 30/3 . . . . *99–100*
765 ILCS 30/4 . . . . *100*
765 ILCS 30/5 . . . . *100*
765 ILCS 30/6 . . . . *100–101*
765 ILCS 30/7 . . . . *101–103*
765 ILCS 30/8 . . . . *103*
765 ILCS 30/9 . . . . *103*
765 ILCS 30/10 . . . . *103*
765 ILCS 33/1 . . . . *103*
765 ILCS 33/2 . . . . *103–104*
765 ILCS 33/3 . . . . . **63–64**, *104*
765 ILCS 33/4 . . . . *104–105*
765 ILCS 33/5 . . . . *105–107*

Page numbers listed in **bold** indicate where the most complete information on a subject can be found. *Italics* indicate pages where the statutes and state-published information pertaining to a subject are located.

765 ILCS 33/6 . . . . *107*
765 ILCS 33/7 . . . . *107*
765 ILCS 33/99 . . . . *107*
Illinois Notary Public
  Handbook *74–111*
Immigration. 26, **53**
  Documents 53
  Fees **47–48**, *92*
  Naturalization
    certificates 53
Impartiality 49
Incomplete documents. **15–16**
                              25, 60–61
                                  64, 111
Insurance, errors and
  omissions. 8

J

Journal of notarial acts. 7, 16
                            40–43, *108*
  Credible identifying
    witness 40, **41–42**
  Disposal 23–24
  Entries, additional 42
  Entries, recommended . . . 41–42
  Signature. 16, **41**
  Signature by mark 50
  Surrender of 42
Jurat (*See* Verification upon
Oath or Affirmation)
  Stamp 7
Jurisdiction **22**

L

Laws pertaining to
  notarization *74–111*
Law, unauthorized practice
  of 17–18, **49–50**, *109*
  Advice. 17–18, **49–50**, *109*
  Assistance 17–18, **49–50**
                                    109
  Blanks in documents 15, **26**
                                    96
  Exceptions **50**, *109*
  Immigration. **53**, *109*

Preparation of
  document 17–18, **26**
                          49–50, *96, 109*
  Selection of document. . . **17–18**
                              49–50, *96*
  Selection of notarization. 45
Legalization (*See* Authentication)
Liability of employer **66**, *97*
Liability of Notary **66–67**, *97*
Liability of surety. **20–21**, *97*
Locus sigilli **44**, 46
Loose certificates 17, **44–45**
L.S. 44, **46**

M

Mark, signature by
  (*See* Signature by mark)
Marriage certificate, certified
copy of 32
Military-officer notarizations 60
  Authentication. 60
  Certificate 60
  Jurisdiction 60
Minors, notarizing for 51
  Age of majority 51
  Identification. 51
  Signature. 51
Misconduct **64–66**, *82, 95–96*
  Advertising, improper foreign-
    language **26**, 52, *90–92*
  Application
    misstatement 3–4, 20, **66**
  Blank affidavit 25, **64**, *95*
  Certificate of
    naturalization 53
  Civil lawsuit. 41, **66–67**
  Felony. 48, **66**, *92*
  Fines. **67**, *98*
  Immigration advice . . 26, **53**, 65
                            82, 90–92, 109
  Influence. 13
  Law, unauthorized
    practice of 45, **49–50**
                            53, 53–54, *109*
  Liability 66–67, *85*, 97

Misdemeanor. 67, *91*, *98*
Naturalization certificate. 53
Official misconduct **67**, *82*
                        98
Overcharging. 48
Revocation of
  appointment **66**, *78*, *98*
Vital record 12, **32**
Willful impersonation. . . . 24, *98*
Misdemeanor (*See* Misconduct)

N

Name change **21**, *77–78*, *93*
National Notary
  Association 128–129
Naturalization certificate. *53*
Nonresident. **19–20**, *84*, *112*
Notarial acts . . . **24–25**, *78–81*, *95*
Acknowledgment. . . . 24, **26–28**
                     78–79, *95*
Affirmation . . .24, **29–30**, *81*, *95*
Authority to notarize 24–25
                         78
Authorized acts 24–25
                     78–81
Choosing. 45
Copy certification by
  document custodian. . . 32–33
Jurat *79–80*
Oath 24, **29–30**, *81*
Proof of execution by
  subscribing witness . . . 24–25
                     35–37, *99*
Unauthorized acts 25–26
Verification upon oath or
  affirmation 24, **30–32**
Witnessing signature 24
                34–35, *80*, *95*
Notarial certificates
(*See* Certificates, notarial)
Notarial record **54–59**, *87–92*
Certificate **58–59**, *89–90*

Contents **56–57**, *88*
Copies. **59**, 65, *90*
Disclosure **59**, *90*
Disposition **58**, *88–89*
Electronic **57–58**
Failure to create. **59**, 65, *90*
Fee **48**, *92*
Form. **58–59**, *89–90*
Retention. **58**, *89*
Thumbprint. **57**, *88*
Notarial wording (*See* Certificates,
  notarial)
Notary seal (*See* Stamp, notarial)

O

Oath 24, **29–34**, 34, 40
                     79–80, *94–95*
Affidavit, for 34
Ceremony 30
Credible identifying
  witness, for **40**, *95*
Credible witness, for 40
Fees **47**, 77, *92*
Gestures 30
Power to administer. 29
Purpose. 29
Response required. 30
Subscribing witness, for 36
Verification 30–32, *79–80*
                       97
Wording 29–30
Oath of office, Notary's 4, **21**
                         85
Filing 4, 21
Requirement 4, 21
Official misconduct 67, *82*
                         98

P

Penalties *67*
Personal appearance 14, 27
                         30, 35

Page numbers listed in **bold** indicate where the most complete information on a subject can be found. *Italics* indicate pages where the statutes and state-published information pertaining to a subject are located.

Personal knowledge
    of identity 14, 27, 28, 30
                31, 36, **37–38**
Photocopies 11
Photographs, notarizing 10
Practices and procedures . . . 37–66
Prohibited acts 25–26, **64–66**
                    82, 95
Proofs of execution by
    subscribing witness 24–25
                    35–37, 99
    Acknowledgment, in
        lieu of 35
    Affirmation 36
    Certificate 36–37
    Fee **47**, 92
    Identification **36**, 78, 109
    Oath 36
    Purpose 35
    Subscribing witness 36
Prothonotary, certificate of
    (See Authentication)

Q

Qualifications for appointment . . .3
                        19–20
Questions and
    answers 107–112

R

Reasonable care **14–18**
                        61–62
Record, notarial (See Notarial record)
Refusal of services 11–12, **61**
Relatives, notarizing for 13, **49**
                        107
Resignation of
    appointment **23–24**, 47
Restricting services 11–12, 61
Revocation of appointment
    (See Misconduct)

S

Satisfactory evidence 37
Scilicet 43

SCT .43
Seal, notarial (See Stamp, notarial)
Secretary of State's office 113
Self-notarization 49
Signature by mark **50–51**, 81
    Certificate 50–51
    Procedure 50–51
    Same as signature 50
    Witnesses **50–51**, 81
Signature(s)
    Certificate 44
    Checking 15
    Journal 16, **41**
    Mark, by **50–51**, 81
    Minor 51
    Notarizing one's own **49**
                        107
    Notary, in presence of . . . **12–13**
                    28, 30, 34–35
    Notary's 17, **44**, 77, 95
Signature witnessing 24
                    34–35, 80, 97
    Certificate 35, 80
    Purpose 34
SS 43
Stamp, jurat 7
Stamp, notarial 5, 6–7, 10–11
                23, 24, 44, **45–47**
                76–77, 86–87
                99–100, 111
    Affixing 5, 17, 44, **46**
    Certificate of
        appointment 4–5, 47
    Disposal of **47**, 111
    Embosser seal 6–7
    Format 6, **46**
    Information required 6, **46**
                        86–87
    Inking stamp 6, **45**, 86–87
    L.S. 44, **46**
    No room for 10–11
    Personal property 46
    Placement 44, **46**
    Requirement **45**, 86
    Smearing 10–11

Wrongful possession **47**, *98*
Stamp, venue 7
Statement of particulars
  (*See* Certificates, notarial)
Statutes pertaining to
  notarization *74–111*
Subscribing witness 36
Supplies 6–8
Surety **20–21**, *76, 85*
                                        94, 97

T

Telephone notarizations. **14**
Term of office,
  Notary's **22–23**, *78, 84*
Testimonium clause
  (*See* Certificates, notarial)
Thumbprint. 7–8, 16, 42, 57
                                88, 90
  Device 7–8
  Notarial record **57**, *88, 90*
  Purpose. 42
Tools, Notary. 6–8

U

Unauthorized acts 25–26
  Blank spaces **25**, *95, 111*
  Blind signers **25**, *96*
  Certified copies **25**, *82*
  Changing documents. . . . **26**, *96*
  Failure to transmit funds *96*
  Foreign language
    advertising **26**, *90–92*
  Immigration expert . . **26**, *90–92*
  Mental illness **25**, *95–96*
  Non-English speaking
    signer **25–26**, *96*
  Preparing documents. . . . **26**, *96*
Unauthorized Practice
  of Law **49–50**
United States Code 60
  10 U.S.C. 936. 60

10 U.S.C. 1044a 60
URPERA 63–64

V

Venue 43
  Stamp 7
Verification upon Oath
  or Affirmation 24, **30–32**
                                79–80, 95
  Affirmation 32
  Certificate **31**, *80, 97*
  Oath 32
  Purpose. 30–31
  Representative capacity 31
Vital records, notarizing 12, **32**
Vital Statistics,
  Bureaus of 120–124

W

Weddings 25
Willingness, determining . . . 14–15
Wills 9, **53–54**
  Advice or assistance. 9
                                53–54
  Living wills 54
Witnessing
  (*See* Signature witnessing)

Page numbers listed in **bold** indicate where the most complete information on a subject can be found. *Italics* indicate pages where the statutes and state-published information pertaining to a subject are located.